Joyce Appleby on *Thomas Jefferson*
Louis Auchincloss on *Theodore Roosevelt*
Jean H. Baker on *James Buchanan*
H. W. Brands on *Woodrow Wilson*
Alan Brinkley on *John F. Kennedy*
Douglas Brinkley on *Gerald R. Ford*
Josiah Bunting III on *Ulysses S. Grant*
James MacGregor Burns and Susan Dunn on *George Washington*
Charles W. Calhoun on *Benjamin Harrison*
Gail Collins on *William Henry Harrison*
Robert Dallek on *Harry S. Truman*
John W. Dean on *Warren G. Harding*
John Patrick Diggins on *John Adams*
Elizabeth Drew on *Richard M. Nixon*
John S. D. Eisenhower on *Zachary Taylor*
Paul Finkelman on *Millard Fillmore*
Annette Gordon-Reed on *Andrew Johnson*
Henry F. Graff on *Grover Cleveland*
David Greenberg on *Calvin Coolidge*
Gary Hart on *James Monroe*
Michael F. Holt on *Franklin Pierce*
Roy Jenkins on *Franklin Delano Roosevelt*
Zachary Karabell on *Chester Alan Arthur*
Lewis H. Lapham on *William Howard Taft*
William E. Leuchtenburg on *Herbert Hoover*
James Mann on *George W. Bush*
Gary May on *John Tyler*
George McGovern on *Abraham Lincoln*
Timothy Naftali on *George H. W. Bush*
Charles Peters on *Lyndon B. Johnson*
Kevin Phillips on *William McKinley*
Robert V. Remini on *John Quincy Adams*
Ira Rutkow on *James A. Garfield*
John Seigenthaler on *James K. Polk*
Hans L. Trefousse on *Rutherford B. Hayes*
Tom Wicker on *Dwight D. Eisenhower*
Ted Widmer on *Martin Van Buren*
Sean Wilentz on *Andrew Jackson*
Garry Wills on *James Madison*
Julian E. Zelizer on *Jimmy Carter*

Parting the Desert: The Creation of the Suez Canal

*A Visionary Nation: Four Centuries of American Dreams
and What Lies Ahead*

The Last Campaign: How Harry Truman Won the 1948 Election

What's College For?: The Struggle to Define American Higher Education

*Architects of Intervention: The United States, the Third World,
and the Cold War, 1946–1962*

Chester Alan Arthur

Zachary Karabell

Chester
Alan Arthur

THE AMERICAN PRESIDENTS

ARTHUR M. SCHLESINGER, JR., GENERAL EDITOR

Times Books

HENRY HOLT AND COMPANY, NEW YORK

Times Books
Henry Holt and Company, LLC
Publishers since 1866
175 Fifth Avenue
New York, New York 10010
www.henryholt.com

Frontispiece: Portrait of President Arthur © Bettmann/CORBIS

Library of Congress Cataloging-in-Publication Data

Karabell, Zachary.
    Chester Alan Arthur / Zachary Karabell.—1st ed.
      p. cm.—(The American presidents)
    Includes bibliographical references and index.
    ISBN-13: 978-0-8050-6951-8
    ISBN-10: 0-8050-6951-8
      1. Arthur, Chester Alan, 1829–1886. 2. Presidents—
United States—Biography. 3. United States—Politics and
government—1881–1885. I. Title. II. American presidents series
(Times Books (Firm))
E692.K37 2004
973.84'092—dc22
[B]   2004041182

First Edition 2004

Printed in the United States of America
5 7 9 10 8 6 4

Contents

Editor's Note

THE AMERICAN PRESIDENCY

The president is the central player in the American political order. That would seem to contradict the intentions of the Founding Fathers. Remembering the horrid example of the British monarchy, they invented a separation of powers in order, as Justice Brandeis later put it, "to preclude the exercise of arbitrary power." Accordingly, they divided the government into three allegedly equal and coordinate branches—the executive, the legislative, and the judiciary.

But a system based on the tripartite separation of powers has an inherent tendency toward inertia and stalemate. One of the three branches must take the initiative if the system is to move. The executive branch alone is structurally capable of taking that initiative. The Founders must have sensed this when they accepted Alexander Hamilton's proposition in the Seventieth Federalist that "energy in the executive is a leading character in the definition of good government." They thus envisaged a strong president—but within an equally strong system of constitutional accountability. (The term *imperial presidency* arose in the 1970s to describe the situation when the balance between power and accountability is upset in favor of the executive.)

The American system of self-government thus comes to focus in the presidency—"the vital place of action in the system," as Woodrow Wilson put it. Henry Adams, himself the great-grandson and grandson of presidents as well as the most brilliant of American historians, said that the American president "resembles the commander of a ship at sea. He must have a helm to grasp, a course to steer, a port to seek." The men in the White House (thus far only men, alas) in steering their chosen courses have shaped our destiny as a nation.

Biography offers an easy education in American history, rendering the past more human, more vivid, more intimate, more accessible, more connected to ourselves. Biography reminds us that presidents are not supermen. They are human beings too, worrying about decisions, attending to wives and children, juggling balls in the air, and putting on their pants one leg at a time. Indeed, as Emerson contended, "There is properly no history; only biography."

Presidents serve us as inspirations, and they also serve us as warnings. They provide bad examples as well as good. The nation, the Supreme Court has said, has "no right to expect that it will always have wise and humane rulers, sincerely attached to the principles of the Constitution. Wicked men, ambitious of power, with hatred of liberty and contempt of law, may fill the place once occupied by Washington and Lincoln."

The men in the White House express the ideal and the values, the frailties and the flaws, of the voters who send them there. It is altogether natural that we should want to know more about the virtues and the vices of the fellows we have elected to govern us. As we know more about them, we will know more about ourselves. The French political philosopher

Joseph de Maistre said, "Every nation has the government it deserves."

At the start of the twenty-first century, forty-two men have made it to the Oval Office. (George W. Bush is counted our forty-third president, because Grover Cleveland, who served nonconsecutive terms, is counted twice.) Of the parade of presidents, a dozen or so lead the polls periodically conducted by historians and political scientists. What makes a great president?

Great presidents possess, or are possessed by, a vision of an ideal America. Their passion, as they grasp the helm, is to set the ship of state on the right course toward the port they seek. Great presidents also have a deep psychic connection with the needs, anxieties, dreams of people. "I do not believe," said Wilson, "that any man can lead who does not act . . . under the impulse of a profound sympathy with those whom he leads—a sympathy which is insight—an insight which is of the heart rather than of the intellect."

"All of our great presidents," said Franklin D. Roosevelt, "were leaders of thought at a time when certain ideas in the life of the nation had to be clarified." So Washington incarnated the idea of federal union, Jefferson and Jackson the idea of democracy, Lincoln union and freedom, Cleveland rugged honesty. Theodore Roosevelt and Wilson, said FDR, were both "moral leaders, each in his own way and his own time, who used the presidency as a pulpit."

To succeed, presidents must not only have a port to seek but they must convince Congress and the electorate that it is a port worth seeking. Politics in a democracy is ultimately an educational process, an adventure in persuasion and consent. Every president stands in Theodore Roosevelt's bully pulpit.

The greatest presidents in the scholars' rankings, Washington, Lincoln, and Franklin Roosevelt, were leaders who confronted and overcame the republic's greatest crises. Crisis widens presidential opportunities for bold and imaginative action. But it does not guarantee presidential greatness. The crisis of secession did not spur Buchanan or the crisis of depression spur Hoover to creative leadership. Their inadequacies in the face of crisis allowed Lincoln and the second Roosevelt to show the difference individuals make to history. Still, even in the absence of first-order crisis, forceful and persuasive presidents—Jefferson, Jackson, James K. Polk, Theodore Roosevelt, Harry Truman, John F. Kennedy, Ronald Reagan, George W. Bush—are able to impose their own priorities on the country.

The diverse drama of the presidency offers a fascinating set of tales. Biographies of American presidents constitute a chronicle of wisdom and folly, nobility and pettiness, courage and cunning, forthrightness and deceit, quarrel and consensus. The turmoil perennially swirling around the White House illuminates the heart of the American democracy.

It is the aim of the American Presidents series to present the grand panorama of our chief executives in volumes compact enough for the busy reader, lucid enough for the student, authoritative enough for the scholar. Each volume offers a distillation of character and career. I hope that these lives will give readers some understanding of the pitfalls and potentialities of the presidency and also of the responsibilities of citizenship. Truman's famous sign—"The buck stops here"—tells only half the story. Citizens cannot escape the ultimate responsibility. It is in the voting booth, not on the presidential desk, that the buck finally stops.

—Arthur M. Schlesinger, Jr.

Chester Alan Arthur

1

A Man of Some Importance

"Chet Arthur? President of the United States? Good God!" It was not exactly what he would have wanted to hear, but then again, it was not exactly the best way to become president. Chester Alan Arthur hadn't wanted to become the nation's chief executive. He certainly hadn't aspired to be vice president—after all, who did? But he had been asked, and he had said yes, never imagining that he would inadvertently set in motion a series of events that would culminate with the assassination of President James A. Garfield and his own elevation to the presidency.

Always an emotional man, Arthur was, by all accounts, devastated by the news that Garfield had been shot on July 2, 1881, by a deranged Charles Guiteau, who has been forever immortalized with the inaccurate moniker of "disgruntled office seeker." Arthur seemed frequently on the verge of tears in the days following, and he prayed as fervently as anyone that Garfield would survive his wounds. It would be nearly three uncertain months before Garfield expired and Arthur became, much to his own shock and that of the nation, the twenty-first president of the United States.

Arthur is one of the forgotten presidents. Mention him to the proverbial man-on-the-street, and blankness is a likely response. "You're writing a biography of who?" was the most common refrain when this particular author mentioned that he was writing about this particular president. Even among those who consider themselves well educated, Chester Alan Arthur remains a cipher, one of those late-nineteenth-century inhabitants of the White House whose echo has been muffled by more memorable individuals and whose footprint—and in the case of the rotund gourmand Arthur a rather large footprint—has been trampled on and all but erased.

Arthur belongs to two select, and not altogether proud, clubs: presidents who came to office because of the sudden death of their predecessor, and presidents whose historical reputation is neither great, nor terrible, nor remarkable. The first club has eight members, and its founder was John Tyler, who replaced William Henry Harrison after the latter died a month into his term. Arthur was the fourth to join, after Andrew Johnson and before Theodore Roosevelt. The second club has a more fluid membership, depending on historical fads and whether or not a new biography has been published that reverses decades of opinion one way or the other. It currently includes Martin Van Buren, Millard Fillmore (who like Arthur also belongs to the first club), Rutherford B. Hayes, Benjamin Harrison, William Howard Taft, Calvin Coolidge, Gerald R. Ford, the first George Bush, and Chester Alan Arthur. It is impossible to remove Arthur from the first club—membership there is permanent. And as to the second, well, maybe, or maybe not. This isn't a long book, but there should be some suspense.

There is a nature-nurture question here. Arthur's time was not conducive to executive action. The White House had shed much of the power it had acquired during the Civil War, and

Congress had asserted its traditional preeminence with the impeachment and near conviction of Andrew Johnson for the unpardonable sin of thinking that he could remove members of his own cabinet without the say-so of the Senate. Given the unelevated state of national politics, many otherwise talented individuals pursued more fruitful outlets for their skills. Why get involved with the rough-and-tumble of statehouses and Congress when fortune beckoned in the West or in industry? Just as the young, hungry, and talented tended to eschew Washington in the 1990s for the seemingly more fertile valleys of silicon, many took one brief look at Gilded Age politics and politicians and opted out.

Henry Adams, the disillusioned sage of the era, famously described the political life of the country after the Civil War in less-than-glowing terms: "The government does not govern. Congress is inefficient, and shows itself more and more incompetent to wield the enormous powers that are forced upon it, while the Executive is practically devoid of its necessary strengths by the jealousy of the Legislature." James Bryce, the English commentator who saw America with at least as much perspicacity as Americans saw themselves, remarked that "an American may through a long life never be reminded of the Federal Government, except when he votes at presidential and congressional elections, lodges a complaint against the post-office, and opens his trunks for a custom-house official on the pier of New York."

Chester Arthur was not well known to the general public before 1880, but he had been collector of the customhouse of the Port of New York. At the time, that was a position of greater influence than all but a handful of federal appointments. The size of the federal government grew rapidly in the 1870s, but the New York Customhouse remained the pinnacle.

It was the largest federal office in the country, and in an era before income tax, it accounted not only for three-quarters of all customs duties but for more than a third of the government's revenues. That the customhouse comprised such a large portion of federal activity simply reflects how much commerce subsumed politics in the late nineteenth century.

While the captains of industry—Rockefeller, Morgan, Frick, Gould, Vanderbilt, Villard, Stanford, Carnegie—carved out empires of wealth in the process of industrializing America, the federal government receded from the center of national attention that it had briefly occupied in the 1860s. Later generations exalted and lambasted the "robber barons," and benignly overlooked the denizens of Washington. As the novelist Thomas Wolfe (the one from Asheville, not Park Avenue) eulogized for the lost generation of American presidents, "Their gravely vacant and bewhiskered faces mixed, melted, swam together in the sea-depth of a past, intangible, immeasurable, and unknowable. . . . And they were lost. For who was Garfield, martyred man, and who had seen him in the streets of life? Who could believe that his footfalls ever sounded on a lonely pavement? Who had heard the casual and familiar tones of Chester Arthur? And where was Harrison? Where was Hayes? Which had the whiskers, which the burnsides; which was which?"

And yet these men did live, and breathe, and think. The newspapers and journals of their day took their actions seriously enough to scorn and ridicule, to praise and assess. They often struck their contemporaries as a questionable assemblage, but there they were, on center stage and playing roles that had consequences. More than most, they added their voices to history. Chester Arthur was an accidental president at an inopportune time, but he is part of the tapestry of who we are more than most ever have been or most of us ever will be.

He was president in an unideological era. The Senate would shortly be dubbed the "Millionaires' Club," and the House of Representatives was an unruly place of loose coalitions and influence trading. State and local politics were controlled by party machines that prized loyalty. Politicians genuflected to the concept of the public good, and they occasionally spoke of public service. But they didn't seem to hold either very dear. Their careers did not depend on bold acts of legislation, stunning moments of oratory, or fighting for an ideal. The years before, during, and immediately after the Civil War had been characterized by an excess of ideology. The politicians of the Gilded Age, perhaps mirroring the mood of the public, turned away from troubling intractables like freedom, democracy, equality, and attended instead to order, stability, and prosperity.

America's cities were growing rapidly. Immigrants flowed into New York and then out into the West, and millions took advantage of the opportunities created by railroads. The dual pressures of burgeoning demographics and industrialization meant chaotic growth. The population of some towns doubled and then doubled again in the span of a decade. In the face of such flux, big ideas took a backseat to daily needs: food, water, shelter, transport, order.

The Civil War resolved the question of slavery that had, in the words of Abraham Lincoln, kept the United States "a house divided," but by the 1870s the memory of the war had begun to recede. Though the Republican Party continued to "wave the bloody shirt" at each presidential convention, hoping to dredge up Civil War passions and eke out an advantage against the better-organized though less popular Democrats, that yielded diminishing returns. In a Gilded Age version of what-have-you-done-for-me-lately, the voting public demanded more than nostalgia for the glorious battles of Gettysburg and Antietam. The Democrats, as one historian noted, stood for "retrenchment and reform." After the drama of war, of radical Reconstruction, and the scandals of the Grant administration, the idea of retrenchment and reform had mass appeal.

Economic expansion created new industries, new jobs, and new voters. For those so inclined, that meant new opportunities for graft. Cities were kept together by political machines, which were tight-knit organizations that corralled votes, collected a percentage of profits, and kept the peace. The machine was epitomized by Tammany Hall in New York City and its majordomo, William Marcy Tweed, a Democratic boss surrounded by a sea of Republicans. More than any mayor, "Boss" Tweed ran New York. His men greeted immigrants as they stepped ashore in lower Manhattan, offered them money and liquor, found them work, and in return demanded their allegiance and a tithe. Supported by Irish Catholics, who made up nearly a quarter of New York's population, Tweed held multiple offices, controlled lucrative public works projects (including the early plans for Central Park), chose aldermen, and herded voters to the polls, where they drunkenly anointed the Boss's candidates. Immortalized even in his own day by the rapier pen of Thomas Nast (has there ever been a political cartoonist who did more to define an era?), Tweed was gone by 1872, forced out and prosecuted, but the system kept going. Every city had its machine, and counties did as well. National politics was simply the apex of the pyramid that rested on local bosses and layers of graft.

It was a system of patronage, first and last. It had been dubbed the *spoils system* earlier in the nineteenth century, because to the victor of elections went the spoils of patronage—jobs could be doled out to supporters in return for their vote come Election Day. In the years after the Civil War, the number of government jobs grew, and so did the spoils system. Even the powerful members of the U.S. Senate were part of the patronage game, because they were not directly elected but instead chosen by the state legislatures, which were themselves an outgrowth of local machine politics. Elections were hotly contested not over principle but over the power of appointment that winning conferred. Senators could appoint a variety of officials at both the federal and state levels. Tens of thousands of jobs were at stake, and these jobs paid salaries, usually quite handsome salaries by the standards of the day. In return for being appointed, officials were expected to make monetary contributions to the party, and their contributions then funded the next round of campaigning.

The contributions were known as *assessments*. There was nothing secretive or shadowy about them. The assessments were set by party leaders, and letters were sent each year and during each election cycle to all salaried civil servants specifying the amount they were expected to contribute. It was a self-perpetuating cycle. Win an election, appoint bureaucrats, judges, administrators, and then use them to pay for the next election. That is why party organizations were so powerful, and why the presidency, even with its executive powers curtailed, remained a plum position. As chief executive, the president had the ultimate power of patronage. Senators decided who would occupy most of the appointments for federal offices in their states, and governors did the same for state officials. But the president of the United States appointed the postmaster general. The postal service, with a branch in every city, town, and village, comprised nearly half the federal bureaucracy, or nearly thirty thousand employees by the 1870s, all of whom could be fired or hired after each presidential election. The president also chose the secretary of the Treasury, who headed the second-largest federal agency, and the one responsible for overseeing the customhouses of major ports such as Boston, Baltimore, and New York.

Jockeying for these offices was intense. Party seniority played a part, but major appointments were also used to reward friends and to penalize foes. Then as now, national parties were loose agglomerations of strange bedfellows, many of whom disliked one another as much as or more than they disliked the opposing party. Midwest Republicans competed with eastern Republicans, West Virginia Democrats with Ohio Democrats, and upstate Buffalo Republicans with New York City Republicans. Within the Republican Party in the 1870s, the major split was between those loyal to Senator Roscoe Conkling of New York and those who followed the lead of Senator James G. Blaine of Maine. The Conkling camp and the Blaine group detested each other, and the mutual animosity of the two senators could hardly have been greater.

Each national election was a patronage contest. Leaders who could most effectively mobilize their networks and raise the most money through assessments tended to emerge victorious, which of course allowed them to consolidate their power and become that much more entrenched. But while government was controlled by a limited number of men, no single group or faction was able to consolidate national power or even create a national base of support. Politics were simply too local, and national parties were at best coalitions of the willing. Even the Democrats, who except for Andrew Johnson were out of the White House from 1860 until 1884, managed to remain competitive with the Republicans because of tenacious local organizations.

There were other issues, to be sure. The railroads that were crisscrossing the continent drew on immigrant labor from China, and in the West those immigrants became the target of resentment and competition. Voices were raised calling for a ban on Chinese immigration, and these got louder year by year. Nascent labor unions developed in the 1870s, and though they sought to extend the rights of the working class, they were sometimes hotbeds of racial intolerance. The 1870s also saw the end of radical Reconstruction in the South and the beginning of a system that was not quite slavery and not quite freedom. The period witnessed the collapse of the economy during the Panic of 1873, and the rise of the temperance movement that would eventually spur both women's suffrage and prohibition. Away from the burgeoning cities of the East, there was an ongoing campaign to pacify the West, as the U.S. Army confronted the Native Americans of the Southwest and those of the vast grasslands of Wyoming, Montana, Kansas, and the Dakotas.

The men in the White House, however, had only tangential influence on these currents. As far as the president was concerned, what mattered most was the steady, stealthy growth of the federal government on the one hand and the quiet evolution of a reform movement against the patronage system on the other. Unexpectedly, the presidency of Chester Alan Arthur was a tipping point. When Arthur entered the White House, he was as closely identified with the political class as any chief executive ever had been. He was what later generations would call the consummate insider, and, as such, he was seen as the least likely reformer of the system that had brought him such rich (in both literal and figurative senses) rewards.

Yet, by the time he left office, he had presided over a sea change in the structure of government. Nixon went to China; Arthur reformed the bureaucracy.

Some would say that he was simply the instrument of forces that had been gestating before him and would have done whatever they did without him, that bureaucratic reform made significant progress under his watch but that he had little to do with it. He certainly wasn't the most active or assertive chief executive, and reform wasn't his idea. So perhaps he was just a placeholder. Which is it? Did reform simply happen while he was president, or did it happen because he was president?

Whatever the answer (and there will be one), Arthur was the sole occupant of the office of president between late 1881 and early 1885, barely remembered even in the early twentieth century, and almost entirely forgotten since then. Given his temperament, and his childhood ambitions, he may not have greatly minded that history has overlooked him. He neither expected nor desired to be president of the United States, and he was as astonished as anyone that he found himself in that role. Given the rapid deterioration of his health barely a year after he left office, his life may even have been cut short because of his service in the White House. In fact, Chester Alan Arthur may have the distinction of being the president who derived the least amount of pleasure from being president. And that is saying a lot, because in his five decades of life before that happened, he took about as much pleasure from life as any of us ever do.

2

The Early Life of Chet

On October 5, 1829, in North Fairfield, Vermont, Malvina Arthur went into labor for the fifth time. The outcome was the successful birth of Chester Alan Arthur. Her husband, the Reverend William Arthur, would not have been in the room but instead might have passed the time reading the Bible, tending to his other four children, and perhaps walking around the porch appreciating the panoply of colors during yet another spectacular New England foliage season. According to local lore, the reverend, lively Irishman that he was, danced around the room when he heard that his wife had given birth to their second son.

The family didn't stay in North Fairfield for long, and like many ministers in the early stages of a career, the Reverend Arthur lived a peripatetic life in search of a permanent parish. As a Baptist minister, he took his family from place to place until he finally found tenure at a church in Union Village, New York, when Chester was ten years old, and then in nearby Schenectady when Chet was fifteen.

The mid–Hudson Valley in the mid-nineteenth century was

a vibrant place; the Erie Canal allowed commerce from the Hudson to make a left turn at Albany and from there head toward Buffalo and the expanding hinterland of the United States. That didn't preclude severe economic downturns. Quite the contrary. The banking system was anarchic and unstable, and booms alternated with busts. Chester Arthur lived through both during his formative years in the orbit of Albany, but his father had a stable income and was able to shield the family from the economic tumult that surrounded them. When Chester was fifteen, he enrolled at Union College in Schenectady, where he remained until 1848. He studied what any undergraduate studied in those years—the Greek and Roman classics in their original, which would have been taught mostly by rote. And as with most undergraduates, Arthur's passion for Homer, Livy, and Cicero was lukewarm at best. According to the few accounts we have, Arthur was an average student in most ways, average in grades and average in his occasional transgressions.

On one issue, however, he was serious and dedicated: slavery. Chester inherited his opposition to slavery from his abolitionist father, who often railed against human bondage from the pulpit. After college, Chester taught for several years, and then in 1854 he became a law clerk at the firm of Erastus Culver, who was one of the leading abolitionist lawyers in New York City. Culver was a staunch opponent of the Fugitive Slave Act, which had been passed as part of the Compromise of 1850 and which required northern states not to shelter slaves who had fled from the South. Opinion in the North was divided. Many New Yorkers and northerners disliked the slave system of the South, but that did not mean they wished to see slavery abolished. Instead, they had a live-and-let-live attitude, and wanted to maintain the half-slave, half-free status quo.

But a status quo can work only when there is stasis. As the country expanded west, the delicate balance was disrupted, and the question of slavery in the territories became the central crisis of the 1850s. In 1854, Congress passed the Kansas-Nebraska Act, which said that the two territories could enter the Union as either a free state or a slave state depending on what their legislatures decided. Though the bill was justified on the noble theory of popular sovereignty, the reality was ugly, as "free-soilers" fought with pro-slavery forces to establish a majority, which would then determine whether the new states would be slave or free. Unlike the more dogmatic abolitionists, free-soilers focused on halting the expansion of slavery rather than on ending it completely. Both were against the institution of human bondage, but the free-soil cause was more pragmatic, and thus appealed to someone like Arthur. Abolishing slavery in the South may have been an admirable dream, but preventing its spread to new states looked like a more realistic and achievable goal. Arthur was so dedicated that he and his law partner Henry Gardiner moved to Kansas themselves in 1856 to lend their support.

Kansas was a violent, divided place, however, and Arthur didn't last long there. The struggle was brutal, and thugs from both sides did their best to terrorize each other. The chaos on the ground was a rude shock to someone whose previous experience had been legal battles in eastern courtrooms. The difference between a pro-slavery ruffian and a free-soil ruffian was nothing compared to the difference between the urbane, educated Arthur and both of them. Frustrated and disoriented, he returned to New York City within months and resumed his practice. He did, however, join the newly formed Republican Party, which had been created to champion the cause of free soil and to give its proponents a national voice.

Back in New York, Arthur built a successful business and found a wife. He met Ellen Lewis Herndon in 1856 and married her in October 1859 at the Calvary Episcopal Church at Fourth Avenue and Twenty-first Street in Manhattan. He doted on her, called her Nell, and set up a home with her nearby, at 34 West Twenty-first Street. His commitment to this neighborhood would last the rest of his life. Even as politics took him to Washington, home was always a small quadrant of Manhattan bounded by Madison Square Park to the north and Union Square to the south. His marriage flourished, as did his practice. Arthur mingled with the elite of the city and was well regarded in Republican circles. Then war broke out.

Arthur flirted with the idea of obtaining a commission in a battlefield unit, but that presented too many complications. Nell's family was from Virginia and, not surprisingly, most of them supported the Confederacy. Civil war between the states was one thing; civil war at home was quite another. Though he did his best to make light of these familial tensions, it was a serious issue. Nell was torn, and already she was beginning to feel constricted by her husband's career. He teased that she was his "little Confederate," or his "rebel wife," and her family deeply disapproved of his ardent support of the Union and the Republicans.

Given his rapid retreat from Kansas several years earlier, Arthur may not have minded staying off the battlefield. His talents as a political animal almost certainly surpassed his skills as soldier. As a young lawyer, he had exhibited a keen sense of how to advance in society. He knew how to make connections with powerful men, including Edwin Morgan, the governor of New York. Through Morgan, Arthur was appointed chief engineer and then quartermaster general for the state, with the

rank of brigadier general. Arthur was responsible for the feeding, housing, and supplying of several hundred thousand
troops, and he proved to be an able manager of this complicated task. He championed an innovative approach to req-
uisitioning. Rather than set up government-run kitchens, he
contracted the work to the lowest bidder, in essence adopting
a free-market approach that saved the government money and
lowered overall costs at a time when the state was strapped
for cash.

During 1861 and 1862, Arthur worked closely with the
governor, and that allowed him to solidify his position in the
all-important patronage network of the New York Republican Party. The fact that he was in daily contact with a cornucopia of material goods and the businesses that provided
them also stoked his materialism and that of his wife. Both of
them appreciated the finer things in life, and as quartermaster,
Arthur earned a healthy living. In an age when many used their
public offices as a source of private enrichment, however,
Arthur did not take advantage of the numerous opportunities
for skimming, and his gains were not ill-gotten. He could easily
have demanded kickbacks from the contracts he awarded. Few
would have objected. As quartermaster, he determined who
would build barracks and for how much; who would provide
uniforms and supplies and for how many. It was almost
expected that the official in charge would take a small cut, but
Arthur did not.

Probity and efficiency notwithstanding, his career as quartermaster was short-lived. He who lives by patronage dies by
patronage, and when the Democrats won the 1862 elections in
New York State, Morgan was out of office and Arthur was
out of a job. The position of quartermaster went to someone

else, and rather than enlist for active duty in combat, Arthur returned to being a full-time lawyer. He parlayed his prior position into a lucrative practice handling contract disputes, including claims of businessmen against the state and federal government for insufficient payment or arrears. While New York City, embroiled in the Draft Riots of 1863, its port teaming with activity, was a rough, tense place in those days, Arthur seems to have carried on his social and professional life untroubled. Mid-nineteenth-century existence in the United States was always beset by some crisis or another. Chaos was normal.

Enmeshed in his work, Arthur did not suffer from the war. His home in Manhattan was lavishly furnished, and it was a hub for dinners and guests. Nell relished being a hostess, though she began to feel increasingly uneasy about the blurring of her husband's social and professional lives and the demands this placed on him in the evening. Arthur knew that his future career depended less on his legal acumen than on his social aptitude. A good lawyer might win cases, but only a well-connected man about town could win the business, and gain the trust, of wealthy and powerful clients. Whether Arthur understood this intuitively or consciously, he clearly grasped that the social scene was his best arena for advancement. He liked people, and they liked him. His cheerful temperament was an asset, especially in an era marked by hatred and division. Arthur had convictions, but he disliked acrimonious arguments and preferred to steer the conversation in less volatile directions. Dinner, drinks, and cigars were not just diversions. They were the tools of Arthur's trade.

Nell remained a devoted wife, though she wanted to see more of her husband. They were both stricken by the death of their first child, William, shortly after the Union victory at Gettysburg. He was two and a half when he died from an infection that caused an inflammation of the brain. As their friends were celebrating General Lee's defeat and the turning of the tide, the Arthurs retreated into deep mourning, and they remained secluded for months.

The victorious end of the war for the North was also a triumph for the Republican Party, and that meant new opportunities for a young Republican such as Arthur. His former patron Edwin Morgan was now a U.S. senator. Just as he had felt more comfortable with the pragmatism of free soil, Arthur did not share the ideological passion of the Radical Republicans then dominant in Washington. Instead, he was part of a circle of more conservative New York Republicans that included William Seward (Lincoln's and Johnson's dyspeptic secretary of state and one of the founders of the party), the elderly Thurlow Weed (the New York Whig-turned-Republican whose patronage power was the stuff of legend), and the party's rising star, Roscoe Conkling.

In 1868, Arthur suffered a setback that was apparent and an advancement that wasn't. Morgan lost his Senate seat (that was the setback), and Conkling gained one (which would prove to be far more advantageous to Arthur in the long run). A stunning six-foot-three-inch peacock, Conkling had served as a congressman before winning the Senate seat, and he was a formidable presence in any room. He strutted his way through Washington, Albany, and New York with the assured confidence of a man who knew that he was destined for greatness. He was born in Albany and spent most of his early years in Oneida County and Utica. Yet he was no rough provincial. He had a penchant for splashy ties and colorful waistcoats, and even during the darkest days of the war he entertained lavishly, whether at the Willard Hotel in Washington, the Fifth Avenue Hotel in New York City, or smaller versions of the similar establishments in Albany or Utica. He cultivated an image of virility, had several high-profile and scandalous extramarital affairs, and was an avid amateur boxer who set up his own private gymnasium in a Washington town house. One journalist observed that Conkling brought the skills of a pugilist to his political bouts. The overall effect was potent, intoxicating, and intimidating. Dubbed "Lord Roscoe" for his impressive hauteur, he also became known as "the Apollo of the Senate," and people often found themselves reaching for Greek and Roman mythology to describe his outsized personality.

Conkling's doppelgänger and archrival in the Republican Party was James Gillespie Blaine, the senator from Maine, who in later years came to be known as the "Plumed Knight." Born and raised in Pennsylvania, Blaine had been a prominent newspaper editor before entering politics, and he served in the House and then the Senate with Conkling. Though both were Republicans, they had a chemical aversion for each other. Blaine delighted in mocking Conkling as a fop and fake, and the thin-skinned Conkling was stung. Blaine proved just as able a street fighter as Conkling, but he was a subtler presence, more reserved and intellectual. He had a solitary quality, and he took solace in a good book. He was also deeply interested in history, and he looked to the past for guidance about America's proper role in the world. Blaine's internationalism was rare for American elites of the day, most of whom looked to the American West as the logical venue for geographic and economic expansion. Blaine looked to Europe, Asia, Africa, and Latin America. It was said that when whiling away hours in his library, he would spin his globe and ponder the state of international relations.

The rivalry between Blaine and Conkling was one of the axes of American politics throughout the 1870s. Those who followed Blaine were called "Half-Breeds," a name first bestowed in derision to mean half-loyal to President Ulysses S. Grant, half-loyal to reform, and fully loyal to none. Soon, however, the label was worn proudly by the Blainites. Against the Half-Breeds stood the "Stalwarts," who had been stalwart in their support for Grant and the patronage system and who were now led by Grant's most passionate advocate, Conkling. Even at the time, the ideological distinction between the two factions was less pronounced than the personal loathing that separated their two leaders.

The Radical Republicanism that defined the immediate years after the Civil War was an attempt by Congress to reengineer the former slave states. The Radicals narrowly failed to remove President Andrew Johnson from the White House via impeachment, and although numerous laws were passed and enforced in the occupied South, their reach exceeded their grasp. The death of the fiery Pennsylvania congressman Thaddeus Stevens in 1868 robbed the Radical wing of the Republican Party of their most potent force, and slowly their influence waned. Stevens's death was followed later that year by the election of Ulysses S. Grant to the presidency. Grant had been a crusty, drunken, charismatic commander, but his presidency marked the end of the politics of passion and the beginning of a long period when personalities determined factions, and when competent, loyal (and at times corrupt) insiders thrived. Grant's defenders described him as an icon of pragmatism necessary to heal the last wounds of the Civil War; his detractors assaulted his administration as a descent into a world where the highest bidder was rewarded.

Grant's inauguration changed the national tenor. Politics in particular and society in general turned away from the fervor that had intensified throughout the 1850s and then exploded in a lethal, destructive war. By the late 1860s, a new generation of Republicans and Democrats jelled into a political class that shared a desire for order and control. In place of stirring orators debating high principles like slavery and federalism, the Senate was occupied by a class of politicos who believed in "women, wine, whiskey, and war," as Senator James McDougall of California remarked. They reveled in the martial cult of the Civil War and eagerly supported America's military expansion westward against the Native Americans of the Plains. But they reveled more in the political machine and its benefits. Conkling defended the machine as a necessary and even constructive force in American political life, thundering, "We are told that the Republican Party is a machine. Yes. A government is a machine, the common-school system of the State of New York is a machine, a political party is a machine. Every organization which binds men together for a common cause is a machine." For him, as for Chester Arthur and even James Blaine, the party was a church to which absolute fealty was expected and demanded, and in emotional moments these men of the machine could wax about its virtues with the romantic zeal of a lover serenading his loved one.

As power passed to a new coterie of Republicans, Arthur benefited. Though his private feelings about Conkling are lost to history, he clearly had a personal affinity for the Stalwart leader. They both had a fondness for the finer things in life, and both were the object of bemused commentary about their tailored clothing and lavish social life. Like Conkling, Arthur spent a small fortune on his wardrobe, which included fine English tweeds for business, frock coats of various hues depending on the season, tuxedos and silken scarfs for the evening, and daily expenses for the maintenance of his hair, burnsides, and whiskers. Both were gentlemen who enjoyed the company of other gentlemen, and whose power derived in no small measure from the influence gained from countless dinner parties, held in mahogany-laden, smoke-filled rooms lit by candlelight. For her part, Nell Arthur took advantage of the perks that her husband's success allowed her and tolerated his frequent absences.

Arthur early on was firmly ensconced in the Conkling camp. But though they were from the same state and shared a love of epicurean delights, they were in other respects quite different. They were the same age, yet Conkling was by far the more forceful personality, the orator who dominated whatever room he was in. Arthur was more subdued, though no less effective a politician. Conkling led, Arthur followed, and they developed a symbiotic relationship. Arthur was best in a supporting role; Conkling followed only himself. Arthur needed to hitch himself to a leader, and Conkling needed someone who was adept at handling people. It was a perfect match.

In 1871, Arthur was offered one of the plum positions in the federal bureaucracy, the collector of the New York Customhouse. He had been earning ten thousand dollars a year as counsel to the New York Tax Commission, when the average salary in the United States barely exceeded five hundred dollars. He was able to augment that income with his private practice, yet the opportunity to serve as collector was not one to pass up. Arthur had quietly established himself as a significant lieutenant in the state party. "His name," said the friendly *New York Times*, "very seldom rises to the surface of metropolitan life, and yet, moving like a mighty undercurrent, this man during the last ten years has done more to mold the course of the Republican Party in this State than any other one man in the county." Arthur, the paper concluded, "was not a brilliant man nor a genius. . . . The secret of his success was his executive ability, and his knowledge of men." The assessment of Arthur's unique gifts was astute, though the paper undoubtedly over-stated his importance in state politics. The *New York Times* was not yet a national paper of record. It was one of several promi-nent New York dailies, and it leaned heavily toward the moder-ate Republican camp defined by Conkling and Arthur.

Arthur was indeed well regarded. He was a genteel, easy-going presence at the customhouse, though no one lauded him for his work ethic. He was late to arrive at his office, early to leave, and he did not administrate with a heavy hand. Nor did he attempt to change the way things were done. The result was that he generated none of the heat that Conkling did, and none of the animosity. The position of collector had opened up when the former occupant, Arthur's friend Tom Murphy, was forced to step down in the face of corruption allegations. Mur-phy had kept close company with the Democrats of Tammany Hall, whose Boss Tweed was himself about to be stripped of power and convicted of defrauding the city, his abuses exposed by adversaries like the Republican editors-turned-crusaders Horace Greeley of the *New York Tribune* and E. L. Godkin of the *Nation*.

If party men like Arthur marked one end of the political spectrum, reformers staked out the other. Reformers were ani-mated by a deep grievance that the Civil War victory over slav-ery and injustice was being squandered. They floated from faction to faction in these years, tolerated but rarely welcome. Half-Breeds embraced them only when it would embarrass the Stalwarts; Democrats included them only when it would hurt the Republicans; and Stalwarts had no interest in them at all.

The pendulum in the 1870s was moving away from causes and hence away from reformers who railed against the spoils system, the corruption of patronage, and the growing inequalities of wealth.

In spirit, the reformers were the direct inheritors of the abolitionist mantle and counted many sermonizing ministers in their midst. They had a tendency to harangue and lecture, and in the age of Grant, not many wanted to listen. They spoke for the plight of immigrants who crowded the cities of the northeastern seaboard. Some looked to the spiritual uplift of the new Americans; others focused on their material well-being. Some reformers organized private charities to aid the poor, but many also looked to change the political system, which they believed had become unfairly rigged to advantage the few at the expense of the many. They railed against graft and corruption in appointments, and that made Tammany Hall and the customhouse prime targets. To them, the postwar party system encouraged the worst excesses: greed, selfishness, pettiness, and a careless disregard for the principles of the Declaration of Independence and the Constitution. Their attempts to shine light on the opaque, and often muddy, political process earned them the scorn of Conkling, who deemed them "man-milliners, the dilettanti, and carpet knights of politics. . . . Their vocation and ministry is to lament the sins of other people. Their stock in trade is rancid, canting self-righteousness. . . . They forget that parties are not built by deportment or by ladies' magazines." That was not all. "When Dr. Johnson defined patriotism as the last refuge of the scoundrel," Conkling announced, "he was unconscious of the then undeveloped capabilities of the word reform." Blaine flirted with the reformers as a way of undermining Conkling. But he was just as devoted to the patronage system, and when his methods were criticized, he too resorted to ad hominem assaults on the manhood of his critics.

Though they were politically marginal, many reformers were also socially prominent, which was one reason for Conkling's scorn. He saw them as men of privilege who were too good to sully themselves with the messy task of governing but whose income and standing in society made them free to criticize and carp. In Boston, Henry Adams and Charles Eliot Norton were from leading families. In New York, Godkin and George William Curtis, both esteemed reformist editors, were members of the elite Century Association, along with Arthur, J. P. Morgan, and the landscape painter Albert Bierstadt. By day, the reformers bitterly denounced what Arthur and Morgan stood for; by night, they all drank together and relaxed in the leathered comfort of libraries marinated in smoke. The high social standing of many reformers meant that their voices were heard, even when they were ignored. And when abuses became too flagrant, or when one faction became too powerful, they could be useful allies. The fall of Boss Tweed and of Murphy, the former collector, were claimed as triumphs by the reformers, but in truth, Tweed was brought down by Republican adversaries who objected more to his influence and reach than to his methods. The reformers could occasionally assist in bringing egregious cases of graft to an end, but for most of the 1870s they were able to do little about the system that made such corruption inevitable.

The problem was that so much of what the reformers detested was legal. The port of New York was the primary gateway for goods from abroad, and smuggling was a constant. Even with a staff of thirteen hundred, the New York Customhouse could not prevent all smuggling, but it did intercept a fair amount. As an incentive, officials who snared illegal, unregistered, or undertaxed shipments were entitled to a percentage of the goods seized or the fines levied. This "moiety" process made it possible for even a low-level official to double or triple his income. Arthur's salary as collector was twelve thousand dollars a year, but his actual income exceeded fifty thousand dollars because of the moiety system, which was many times more than the average salary in the United States at the time.

Even though there was nothing illegal about the moiety system, it struck reformers, and a fair portion of the American public, as unsavory. Why should a few lucky civil servants, appointed because they knew the right people, personally benefit from laws meant to serve the public good? Though Grant easily won reelection in 1872 against the well-intentioned but politically inept reformer Horace Greeley, popular sentiment favored some nod in the direction of reform. While it was true that the political class often acted with little thought for the public, voter sentiment could not be completely ignored, and voter anger was something even the most arrogant congressman or state official feared.

The Panic of 1873, caused by the bankruptcy of the Northern Pacific Railroad and the collapse of Jay Cooke's powerful brokerage house, resulted in financial devastation and widespread unemployment. The economic depression severely weakened the case of those elected officials who argued for the status quo. The reformers adeptly used the furor caused by the panic to engineer reform. They were overrepresented in journalism and in the pulpit, and they were able to use those forums to demand an end to the moiety system. With millions uncertain about where their next meal was coming from, it didn't look good that some civil servants were becoming extremely wealthy. In 1874, Congress passed the Anti-Moiety Act, which ended the practice of legal personal gain from seizures. The result for Arthur was dramatic: his income dropped almost 80 percent, back to his base salary of twelve thousand dollars. He was still a rich man but no longer an embarrassingly overpaid one.

Grant chose not to run for a third term in 1876, and the Republican nomination initially seemed to belong to James Blaine. Conkling also jockeyed for the nomination, but outside of New York and Pennsylvania, his candidacy did not have national momentum. The Stalwarts were united only by Grant, and Conkling had enemies even within the Stalwart camp. Blaine, however, was the unquestioned leader of the Half-Breeds, and he was as good a machine politician as there was. Even so, his prospects were derailed by an insidious bit of political sabotage. Letters were revealed that raised doubts about his integrity during a railroad deal gone sour some years before. There was nothing uncommon about politicians in the late 1860s and 1870s taking a stake in the speculative and potentially lucrative railroad business, but more often than not, railroads swallowed investments and went bankrupt. While Blaine was able to keep the full contents of the potentially damaging letters from becoming public, his position was weakened going into the Republican National Convention that summer, and instead, Governor Rutherford B. Hayes of Ohio was nominated as the party's candidate on the seventh ballot.

Against Hayes, the Democrats nominated Samuel Tilden, the reformist governor of New York. The capacity of the "bloody shirt" to rouse the Republican faithful hadn't completely evaporated, but it was losing its visceral power. The Democrats could and did run on a platform of cleaner, more efficient government after eight years of a Grant administration that had seen a succession of scandals and a dearth of meaningful legislation. Tilden had been part of a remarkable revival of the Democratic Party in New York. He had led the charge against Boss Tweed and against corruption, even though Tweed was a Democrat. He had skillfully taken advantage of the Republican disdain for Irish Catholics and other marginal groups and assembled a coalition based on populism and reform.

For the Republicans, Hayes was a superior choice because he was personally untainted by the more repellent aspects of the Grant administration and the spoils system and could make a stand against Tilden on the grounds of good government. But he still wanted to win, and that meant taking full advantage of the assessment system that required all Republicans in state and federal government to contribute money to the campaign.

Though Arthur and Conkling had worked to prevent Blaine's nomination, they were not fans of Hayes. They were, however, good party men, and they did all they could to ensure the Ohio governor's victory in New York and throughout the country. The election of 1876 produced the most controversial outcome in American history, at least until the election of 2000. Tilden won the popular vote, but three southern states elected two sets of electors, one Democrat and one Republican, and the result was deadlock. If the Republican electors were used, Hayes would win. If not, the White House would go to Tilden. After months of brinkmanship and negotiation, a special congressional committee seated the Republican electors, and Hayes was declared the winner. He was duly sworn into office on March 5, 1877, but he never escaped the sobriquet of "His Fraudulency."

In his inaugural address, the new president pointedly identified civil service reform as the centerpiece of his agenda—and not just symbolic reform but changes that would be "thorough, radical, and complete." That was not welcome news to the Stalwarts or to the Half-Breeds, and Conkling did not appreciate the message. He was even less enthused by Hayes's cabinet, which was stocked with liberal, reformist Republicans such as Senator Carl Schurz of Missouri as secretary of the interior and Ohio's Senator John Sherman (William Tecumseh Sherman's younger brother) at the Treasury. Conkling could live with token symbols of reform in the cabinet, but not with the reality of reform implemented by the White House. In the spring of 1877, Hayes noted in his diary, "Now for civil service reform. Legislation must be prepared. . . . We must limit and narrow the area of patronage. We must diminish the evils of office-seeking." Strong words, followed by strong action. Secretary of the Treasury Sherman launched an investigation of corrupt practices at the major customhouses in the United States and appointed John Jay, the grandson of the first chief justice of the United States, to head a commission specifically targeting New York. And with that, Chester Arthur, who had kept a relatively low profile in spite of his lofty position, suddenly became the center of a national crisis.

3

Onto the National Stage

There was no shortage of allegations: illegal kickbacks, over-staffing, insidious accounting, and lax administration were only a few of them. But Chester Arthur had never before been the target of an investigation and had maintained a benign reputation. At worst, he was seen as a party hack, but no one had seriously challenged his probity, until now.

Much like Conkling, Arthur was seen as part of a corrupt system rather than corrupt himself. He had taken advantage of moiety kickbacks, true, but he had stayed within the system. Oddly enough, that had made him acceptable to the reformers, and it was one reason why he had been reappointed to an unprecedented second term as collector in 1875. Because he was marked, and rightly so, as a man who would bend with the prevailing winds, he was not a primary target of reformist zeal. In fact, he was often lauded by the New York press as a likable individual who did his best to remain honorable in a dishonorable profession. The *New York Times*, admittedly partisan to the Stalwarts, complimented Arthur as a model of efficiency who had the added advantage of being kind and respectful to his subordinates.

His good reputation notwithstanding, the charges raised by the Jay Commission were severe. As one advocate of reform in 1877 commented: "If we turn to Collector Arthur, we find some improvement on the old order of things, but much which is a continuation of it. . . . We read the old story of political assessments: that one man last year paid sums amounting to $100, $200, and $300; . . . that under the present system, the officers who are appointed through political influence are expected to make their offices contribute to the support of the party. . . . We read of clerks receiving three or four hundred dollars beside their salaries; of weighers who are never seen on the docks, while their assistants come late, leave early, and read the papers; of men who are deficient in a proper attention to business as well in business qualifications and character." Yet Arthur himself was not directly implicated; instead he was charged with looking the other way. He was also criticized for tardiness, on the grounds that he often didn't arrive at work until noon. On that score, he was guilty.

The Jay Commission submitted a fairly damning report, and Secretary Sherman instructed Arthur to reduce the number of employees and to institute more rigorous hiring qualifications and administrative practices. Too many people, the Jay Commission reported, were hired solely on "the recommendations of their friends." The defenders of the spoils system found that charge absurd, not because it was false but because that was the whole point. Appointees were supposed to be friends of the faction in power. That was what made them appointable and what guaranteed that they would contribute to the party's coffers. Granted, assessments were supposed to be paid out of salaries, yet the Jay Commission found that they were instead being charged against the operating budget of the government. That wasn't right, but in the eyes of the Stalwarts, neither was the president's reaction. Hayes issued an order forbidding federal employees from providing assessments in subsequent elections. The Stalwarts denounced the move, but the reformers still weren't satisfied and pressured Hayes to do more. In September, the president made the decision to break with Conkling and the Stalwarts and ordered Sherman to remove Arthur as collector. Conkling, who hadn't minded some nods in the direction of reform, was now enraged.

The senior senator from New York was not Arthur's sole defender. Edwin Morgan, Arthur's first patron, wrote to Hayes protesting the decision. "Gen'l Arthur is entitled, on his merits, to remain til the expiration of his term. . . . He is strong and popular with the merchants and business men of both parties. He is an able lawyer, an excellent man of business, kind and generous to all, and liberal in furnishing the sinews of war." Hayes replied that he wanted a new collector to "implement the recommendations and reforms of the Jay Commission," and he did not believe Arthur was capable of doing so. Hayes may have been genuine about the need for reform, but he also wanted to break the hold of the Stalwarts over the national Republican Party. In response, Conkling declared war.

Lord Roscoe drew on a smorgasbord of tactics. He challenged the president's right to remove Arthur on the same grounds that had been used to impeach President Johnson ten years before, the Tenure of Office Act. Conkling claimed that Hayes had violated the cherished tradition of senatorial courtesy that demanded a president not take action against a political appointee unless the senators from that person's state concurred, and he marshaled the Senate to oppose Hayes. Almost as an afterthought, he also defended Chester Arthur as a man above rebuke.

Arthur wisely let others fight for him. Even so, he was not

silent and occasionally fired off angry, righteous letters reminding both friend and foe that no charges had been levied against him specifically. In December 1877, the Senate voted to reject several of Hayes's nominees, including the man nominated to replace Arthur: Theodore Roosevelt, Sr., a wealthy, liberal Republican remembered for his even more successful son. Arthur was relieved and triumphant. He wrote to Conkling expressing his thanks. "I cannot tell you how gratified I am at the splendid victory you have won—apart from & way beyond any personal considerations of my own. The whole town is excited by the event & the current of popular feeling is all with you."

Hayes had been humiliated. The reformers were disgusted with him and whispered that he was weak. Conkling and the Stalwarts strutted through the Christmas season. Hayes had two options: he could suffer the defeat and all but concede that power had passed out of the White House and into the hands of the Senate, or he could fight. He chose the latter, and he wisely bided his time. After several months, he again turned on Arthur, and this time he outmaneuvered the Stalwarts.

Throughout the spring, Washington and New York buzzed with rumor and innuendo that Arthur had flouted the administration and refused to implement the recommendations of the Jay Commission. The correspondence between Arthur and Sherman was leaked to the press, and Hayes's allies took every opportunity to contrast Arthur's actions with the steps outlined in the late fall of 1877. Arthur rebuked his critics and defended his record, announcing that he was gradually reducing staff and punishing misconduct but that such matters had to be done carefully and diligently lest innocent, honorable civil servants get caught in the dragnet. Hayes, however, was not listening. It was no longer a matter of what Arthur did. His very presence was an affront, and when Congress went into summer recess in 1878, Hayes again instructed Sherman to suspend Arthur along with the city naval officer Alonzo Cornell and replace them. This time, it was permanent.

The *New York Times* defended Arthur's tenure as collector, saying that during his time "the New York Customhouse [was] the most investigated place in the country, but it has come out from each ordeal without a single breath of allegation against its head." The *Times* insinuated that the true reason for Arthur's dismissal was that he had been more loyal to his staff than to the incoming administration and therefore refused to pack the customhouse with Hayes's appointees. It was a brilliant counterstroke: accuse the administration of acting not for reform but for venal patronage, which meant that the Hayes administration occupied the lower circle of Hell reserved for hypocrites.

Rather than ruining Arthur's career, Hayes's vendetta catapulted him to national attention. He became the darling not just of the Stalwarts but of a motley assortment of the administration's opponents. Though Arthur was removed, the imbroglio was kept alive by newspapers, by congressional committees, and by state nominating conventions, which used the confrontation as the axis for other debates. The Democrats in Washington veered toward Arthur and Conkling because they recognized the issue would divide the Republican Party and give the Democrats a better chance at capturing the White House in 1880.

In the end, the Senate decided in February 1879 not to overturn Hayes's decision and confirmed a new collector, the liberal Republican Edwin Merritt, to oversee the vast revenue that flowed through the New York Customhouse. Arthur once again took up his law practice and was awarded by Conkling with the position of chairman of the New York Republican Party. The Hayes administration did indeed staff the custom-house with friendlier appointees who could then act as a crucial source of income and support during the next election. Meanwhile, the midterm elections of 1878 had given the Democrats control of both the House and the Senate, which placed Hayes in the unpleasant position of fighting against a powerful Congress controlled by the other party. The Stalwarts, for their part, could not have been more pleased at Hayes's predicament.

Arthur's state of mind during this period can only be guessed. Most of his papers were destroyed at his death. But it's likely that in spite of the furor over his removal as collector, these years were among the happiest in his life. He was wealthy; he was happily married; he was engaged in work he cared about on behalf of a party he loved; and he enjoyed the ironclad support of one of the most powerful politicians in the country. He worked energetically on behalf of the New York Republican Party, and one of his central tasks as party chairman was the social massaging that accompanied fund-raising.

His two foci were the New York state elections in 1879 and the preparations for the Republican National Convention in Chicago in 1880. Arthur was responsible for getting out the vote for Stalwart candidates, and that meant money and organization. He wrote countless letters to state and federal employees who owed their careers to the Stalwarts, and requested that they contribute a certain amount to the party funds. While phrased as requests, these letters were actually orders, or invoices. The recipient was obligated to pony up, and Arthur was both a successful fund-raiser and a persistent one. In part due to his efforts, the Conklingites swept the 1879 state elections, thereby solidifying the senator's position as a power broker in the national Republican Party.

Arthur, meanwhile, delighted in the soft aspects of the job. Then as now, party officials went from one banquet to another, eating meal after meal with a revolving door of donors and would-be appointees. Arthur had a particular predilection for this work, and Nell was a superb partner. Both she and Chet doted on their children: son Chester Alan, whose birth had followed William's premature death during the war, and daughter Ellen, named after her mother. Nell organized frequent dinners, music recitals, and parties at their home at 123 Lexington Avenue, and she kept meticulous notes about who was who in New York society, especially in Republican society. As the Arthur biographer Thomas Reeves noted, she was ambitious for her husband, and she treated their social life as a career of her own.

As friends later acknowledged, however, she would have been happier if Chester had made their home the center of his life. Instead, it was only one of his haunts, and not the preferred one. There were few things that he enjoyed more than wining and dining in the company of like-minded men. He conducted business from his offices in the Fifth Avenue Hotel, within walking distance of 123 Lexington. Today, the only trace of Arthur's presence in the neighborhood is a statue of him, standing quietly on a pedestal at the northeast corner of Madison Square Park at Twenty-sixth Street. But at the time, the Fifth Avenue Hotel was the epicenter of New York Republican politics, the Waldorf-Astoria of its day. It was a mishmash of wood paneling, chandeliers, neoclassical touches, heavy drapery, and cigar smoke. And it was Arthur's second home.

When he wasn't entertaining there, he could often be found at Delmonico's Restaurant, also on Fifth Avenue. As the hub of elite society gravitated to Fifth Avenue north of Washington Square Park, Delmonico's, an old downtown café, moved uptown and went upscale. In 1876, having relocated to Fifth Avenue and Twenty-sixth Street, the restaurant defined a new level of opulence. It was vast, occupying most of the block between Broadway and Fifth Avenue, and it was expensive. It had main rooms, ballrooms, and private rooms. Silver chandeliers hung from mosaic-covered ceilings. Mirrors were everywhere—rich, heavy, gilded mirrors—and there was a central courtyard with a fountain. "The service," said a reviewer for the *New York Tribune,* "[is] splendid. The waiters as noiseless as images in a vision. . . . The dishes succeed each other like the well-composed tones of a painting or a symphony." Yes, even the food was good, which was hardly common in those days of bad knockoffs of heavy Cordon Bleu cuisine.

Delmonico's was where political and business elites met and mingled. Food, drink, and decor were the lures, and the restaurant fulfilled a vital social function. Until he became president, Chester Arthur used the Fifth Avenue Hotel and Delmonico's as his offices. They were where he met with the Astors and the Goulds, the Morgans and the Conklings, the patrons and the robber barons. They were where promises were exchanged; where donors pledged money; where candidates were selected. They were where power was.

The contrast between Arthur's stomping grounds north of Union Square and those of the masses to the south was staggering. As the population of New York City grew in the nineteenth century, the city marched north from lower Manhattan. The city's fortunes were inextricably linked to the nearly two hundred docks and wharves that made a horseshoe around the southern part of the island. Across the East River, Brooklyn was a teeming city in its own right, with its own warehouses stocked with goods and its own problems. But New York was of a different order entirely. By the 1870s, the city had nearly a million inhabitants, though no one knew for sure exactly how many immigrants lived in the tenements and hovels that spread out from Five Points east of the Bowery and south of Cooper Union. There, as many as 250,000 people were crammed into a square mile. Sewage ran in muddy ditches through the narrow streets, and people competed with horses and carts and usually lost. Navigating through the labyrinth was a constant challenge, and it was easy to get lost in the dark of night. The mix of animal feces and human waste was a recipe for disease, and New York had the highest death rate of any city in the Western world.

The only common ground was Central Park, which was not yet complete in the 1870s but which would soon become the city's melting pot. When he was collector, Arthur passed near to the tenements to get to his office at the customhouse, but it's not clear that people of his class really noticed how most people in the city lived. Arthur's home and Delmonico's were less than a mile north of the tenements, but they were a world away.

In the city and throughout the country, trade unions were just beginning the struggle to carve out a larger slice of economic rewards for workers. Women were starting to question the limited scope of their political rights. Railroads were crisscrossing the continent, making a steel baron named Andrew Carnegie richer than all his Scottish relatives combined and a few New York bankers wealthy and most investors very, very poor. New inventions proliferated, especially at the hands of Thomas Alva Edison, and 124,672 new patents were issued in the 1870s, more than double the decade before. Hayes was the first president to have a telephone in the White House, though its use was still limited compared to the telegraph. Mail-order catalog businesses thrived with the expanding U.S. Post Office, and though that led Anthony Comstock, the postmaster general, to issue directives banning the use of the post for the transport of any materials he deemed to be obscene, it also led to a boom for the retail trade.

The country had nearly 50 million people, and while some gloried in the rapid changes, many felt dislocated. Reformers looked for things to reform but often despaired that they were tilting at windmills. Henry George, the best-selling author of *Progress and Poverty* (1879), proposed a single tax based on land ownership that would redistribute wealth away from the 1 percent of the population who owned more than 90 percent of the country's wealth and offset the destructive imbalances caused by the yawning gap between rich and poor. George was especially troubled by the corruption and sprawl of urban America and asked a friend what could be done. "Nothing," his friend replied, "you and I can do nothing at all. We can only wait for evolution." That was not a satisfying answer, but the prospects for change seemed daunting. Every night, the gilded elite gathered at Delmonico's to declaim against the likes of Henry George. It was their world, and one of its stewards was Chet Arthur.

Neither Arthur nor his peers were in any danger of being stripped of their wealth, but they had no defense against disease. Just as he was reaching the pinnacle of success, Arthur lost something precious: his wife. Nell Arthur died suddenly of pneumonia, at the age of forty-two, just after New Year's Day 1880. Arthur was devastated. He had loved her, but he had also spent more evenings apart from her than with her. Though she had not been content with her husband's life outside of their home, she had never been anything but cheerful and supportive of him in public. Arthur was visibly distraught for weeks, and even into the spring he seemed subdued.

The Republican National Convention was approaching, however, and that gave Arthur something to occupy his time and energy. The plan for the Stalwarts was to nominate Ulysses S. Grant for a third term. Grant remained immensely popular to the Republican base, and although his eight years as president had been characterized by cronyism and corruption, the Stalwarts preferred him to Hayes and especially to Blaine, who appeared to have the edge going into the convention. Grant, it was widely remarked, stood for nothing but himself. No program, idea, or platform was associated with his name, and his appeal lay in the fact that he was seen as a potential unifier of a fragmented party.

But Blaine wasn't interested in joining a Grant bandwagon driven by Conkling and Arthur. He wanted the nomination for himself. That made the New York Republicans even more stalwart in their support for Grant, and when the convention assembled in Chicago in June 1880, Arthur was at the helm of his state's delegation.

Nominating conventions were raucous, unpredictable affairs. The betting action outside Exposition Hall was nearly as intense as the balloting inside it. The convention began deadlocked between Grant and Blaine, and remained that way for thirty-five ballots. Treasury Secretary John Sherman (who had removed Arthur from the customhouse) made a showing, but he was considered barely viable. As for Hayes, he had alienated too many of his former supporters. Given the vagaries of machine politics and party dynamics, the fact that he was president was not enough to guarantee his renomination. He removed himself from consideration before the convention, but he would have faced a hard road had he tried to run again. Though presidents controlled a substantial network of patronage, they did not control the party, and Hayes was neither the first nor the last sitting president not to be renominated.

With each successive ballot, the prospects for the two front-runners faded as well. The Stalwarts and the Half-Breeds were so antagonistic that neither camp would break ranks for the other, and it became clear that neither Grant nor Blaine would be able to command the necessary two-thirds majority of the delegates.

The result was the emergence of a dark-horse candidate, James A. Garfield, who was in the convention hall as a member of the Ohio delegation. Garfield had been a general during the Civil War and then served eighteen years as a congressman. He was universally respected by those who knew him, and he elicited a neutral response from most of the party. He was known as a moderate and had shown no signs of overweening ambition. Indeed, he had given the nominating speech for John Sherman. Neither a Stalwart nor a Half-Breed nor a Hayes man, on the thirty-sixth ballot he became the Republican nominee for president.

Almost immediately, Garfield had to select a vice presidential running mate who would be put to the convention for a vote. Conkling was upset that Grant hadn't won, but he was pleased that Blaine had lost. The story of how Chester Arthur came to be Garfield's choice was told almost thirty years later by a reporter named William Hudson. It is the only account of the tense discussions that took place between Arthur and Conkling, and there is no way of confirming its veracity. But it was juicily written and has been irresistible to biographers and chroniclers, including this one. According to the report, Garfield's partisans settled on Arthur's name as an unobjectionable sop to the Stalwarts. Garfield could not win New York without them, and he would be hard-pressed to win the election if he lost New York. Arthur was firmly identified with the Stalwarts, and he was almost universally liked within the Grand Old Party.

Conkling, however, was in no mood to see his lieutenant vaulted above him. While no one coveted the vice presidency, it was still a national office with national prestige, and Conkling preferred to extract promises of patronage. He may also have been concerned that if Arthur accepted, Garfield would act as if he owed nothing more to the Stalwarts. But tactical and strategic quibbles were secondary. What most annoyed Conkling was the blow to his pride. Arthur was approached directly by the Garfield camp. Conkling was not asked first and did not learn about the idea until Arthur informed him.

"The Ohio men have offered me the vice presidency," Arthur told Conkling in a quiet back room of the convention hall.

"Well, sir," Conkling is said to have replied, "you should drop it as you would a red hot shoe from the forge."

To Conkling's apparent astonishment, he did not. "The office of the vice president," Arthur answered stoutly, "is a greater honor than I ever dreamed of attaining." Conkling responded that Garfield was going to lose the election, and that the Stalwart day would come in 1884. He could not imagine why Arthur would want to jettison a promising future on a losing ticket. But Arthur saw it differently. "A barren nomination would be a great honor. In a calmer moment you will look at this differently," he said.

"If you wish for my favor and my respect you will contemptuously decline it," Conkling answered.

"Senator Conkling," Arthur shot back, "I shall accept the nomination and I shall carry with me a majority of the delegates." Startled into speechlessness, Conkling turned and walked out of the room.

The specific words may be apocryphal, but the shift in Arthur and Conkling's relationship was anything but. Given Conkling's personality, he could not have reacted with equanimity to Arthur's elevation, and he must have realized that the guard was changing. In fact, in the moments just after Garfield's victory and Blaine's defeat, Conkling reached the apex of his influence. The moment Arthur was nominated, Conkling's star began to wane, and within slightly more than a year he ceased to be a power broker and Arthur was president.

That was not an outcome anyone would have predicted in the summer of 1880. After Arthur was confirmed by the delegates, the convention broke up, and the essayists drew their stilettos. "The nomination of General Garfield," observed *Harper's Weekly*, "has been received with great satisfaction by Republicans throughout the country. . . . [But] Mr. Arthur was selected in accordance with the principle which governs the practice of nominating conventions—to placate the minority." John Sherman, smarting from his own defeat and from the stunning elevation of a man he had recently fired, said that Arthur running for vice president was "a ridiculous burlesque." Harvard's Charles Eliot Norton called the choice of Arthur "a miserable farce." And the *Nation* wryly editorialized that the nomination of Arthur might just convince Conkling to make one stump speech on behalf of the ticket. The nominee was notably undistinguished, the magazine's editor, E. L. Godkin, wrote the following week, but he urged readers not to worry.

"General Garfield, if elected, may die during his term in office, but that is too unlikely a contingency to be worth making extraordinary provisions for."

In the space of less than two years, Chester Arthur had gone from being the best-paid employee of the federal government to a well-remunerated lawyer and head of the New York Republican Party to vice presidential nominee. He had escaped one cauldron only to jump into another. Even his Panglossian temperament must have been tested by the scorn that greeted his nomination. He had lived an oddly insulated public life and had thrived within it. That was about to change. Arthur knew that and dreaded it. He left Chicago as quickly as possible and went home. A crowd had assembled at Grand Central depot in Manhattan to celebrate his arrival, but his friends, who understood Arthur's preference to be out of the public limelight, had him led out a side door and into a carriage so that he could, as his sister Regina explained in a letter, "have a chance to rest for one night . . . and to eat his dinner." But as pleased as he was to be home, she confessed, he could not stop himself from breaking down in tears as he remembered the wife who wasn't there to share his good fortune. The next night, the crowd came to him and essentially forced him to celebrate publicly, which he did politely but unenthusiastically.

After a brief respite, Arthur turned his energies to the election. The Republican Party platform made an anodyne nod in the direction of civil service reform, as did the Democratic platform, which was written under the aegis of party nominee General Winfield Scott Hancock, another Civil War hero, and his running mate, former congressman William English of Indiana. Garfield was favored by the reform wing of the Republican Party because he seemed to eschew the naked system of patronage and promised that he would, if elected, be beholden to no one. Would that it had been so. Garfield might have wanted, in an ideal world, to run a campaign untainted by the association with professional politics, but in the real world, he wanted to win. That presented him with a choice: lose honorably or win less honorably. And as the nominee of the Republican Party for president of the United States, that wasn't really a choice at all.

4

———

To the White House

The campaign of 1880 is notable mostly for what it lacked. It was a contest of organization and will, not a battle over the future direction of the country. The Republican factions in Chicago were divided by personalities, not by beliefs, and the Democrats did not offer a dramatically different vision. Within each party, there were voices calling for reform and lamenting the retreat from ideals, and outside both parties protest movements gestated. Feeling that their needs were being overlooked, farmers and workers were beginning to organize, and in 1880 the Greenback Party nominated another Civil War general, James B. Weaver of Iowa, to run for president on behalf of the dispossessed and disenfranchised.

But the main attraction had all the ideology of a horse race. That fact did not escape the disgusted intellectuals who sat on the sidelines wondering what had happened to the once noble republic of Washington, Jefferson, and Lincoln. To Henry Adams, E. L. Godkin, and others, Stalwart, Half-Breed, Democrat, and Republican were all arbitrary labels that could easily have been shuffled without altering anything but the names of the combatants. They had a point. What was the election about, really, other than who would win? There were debates and questions in 1880, debates about suffrage and Western expansion and tariffs, questions about immigration and labor and civil service reform, but few people voted for Garfield-Arthur or for Hancock-English on the basis of where the two parties stood on those issues. They voted because of party loyalty or because some local organizer sweetened the pot. They voted because a Republican precinct boss in New York or Boston or Pittsburgh or a Democrat in Buffalo or St. Louis or Nashville invited them to a picnic on a fine Sunday in September, trucked out a few respected and/or dynamic speakers, and handed out whiskey, beer, and dollar bills.

Yet if you had collared Garfield and Arthur or Hancock and English and asked them if they stood for anything, they would of course have said yes. They would have said they stood for good government, for the hopes and dreams of the common man, for the expansion of trade, for orderly cities and prosperous farms, well-managed railroads, solvent banks, stable currency, and the settlement of the West. Having served the Union during the Civil War, they felt that the North's victory had closed the last great fissure that had threatened a country founded on principles of liberty, freedom, and the pursuit of happiness. It wasn't that they eschewed ideology; it wasn't that they were all venal or cynical. They believed, simply, that everyone would be best served by a government led by their faction.

After decades of ideological strife, the postwar generation of politicians viewed order as the most important public good. Political appointments and party discipline helped ensure order nationally, and if party leaders stood to gain from electoral success, all the better. Most politicians of the era saw no inherent conflict between government service and personal gain. They would have looked at later generations of Americans, at the reformers of the twentieth century who created one box for public service and a separate one for private advancement, and scoffed at the naïveté. Most politicians of the 1870s and 1880s looked at government as a vehicle for both. Accusations that they were feeding at the public trough made minimal sense to them. Government was an institution for the public good that was meant to reward those who entered it.

No one described the mix of sublime and mundane better than the Republican senator from Kansas, John Ingalls. In an era when man's conquest of nature was proceeding in an uninterrupted stampede, when the wonders of evolution and the fate of dinosaurs were occupying the salon dreams of the educated and the elite, Ingalls let loose a rhetorical fancy that almost flew away from him in a flurry of flowery verbiage. Government circa 1880, he remarked, "can properly be regarded as in the transition epoch and characterized as a pterodactyl. . . . It is, like that animal, equally adapted to the waddling and dabbling in the slime and mud of partisan politics, and soaring aloft with discordant cries into the glittering and opalescent empyrean of civil service reform."

In an age before television or radio, only a small part of a presidential campaign was waged by the candidates themselves. Garfield and Arthur could personally reach only a fraction of the electorate. Instead, they relied on hundreds of others to speak for them throughout the country. Organizing events and obtaining speakers were crucial components for victory, and that required money and managers. Arthur was a brilliant fundraiser and a persuasive manager, and he was a central factor in the eventual victory.

The first order of business was reconciliation. Political parties often emerge from their convention bruised and fragmented. One moment the aspirants for the nomination are attacking each other; the next they're expected to make nice and work for the common goal of electing the party's nominee. Conkling left Chicago with a strong disinclination to help Garfield, and he needed and expected to be courted. Arthur helped arrange a meeting between Garfield and Conkling, to be held at the Fifth Avenue Hotel in early August 1880. It was a tricky assignment. Conkling, naturally, wanted explicit concessions and guarantees of influence and appointments. Garfield wanted to promise as little as possible in order to maintain his image as a man above faction.

But Garfield could not win without the Stalwarts. They controlled too much patronage, and the New York group was linked to the coffers of rich and powerful railroad barons like Jay Gould and bankers such as J. P. Morgan. As a gesture of goodwill, Garfield traveled by rail from Mentor, Ohio, to New York via Buffalo, and he made more than a dozen stops along the way to meet, greet, and speak. He arrived in New York on a steamy August 4. The so-called Fifth Avenue Conference convened the following day, with one rather odd twist. "Senator Conkling," wrote the *New York Times*, "was conspicuously absent."

Whether it was a callous snub or a calculated reminder of power, Conkling's no-show put his supporters in a bind. Somehow, Arthur and fellow New York Republican Thomas Platt (who described the meeting in his autobiography) managed to make excuses for the Stalwart leader and continue what had become a somewhat surreal exercise: a high-profile summit with only one of the two disputants present. Garfield left New York even less fond of Lord Roscoe, and he noted in his diary that "the absence of Conkling gave rise to unpleasant surmises about his attitude," and that Arthur and Platt were "embarrassed and somewhat indignant." When the meetings concluded the next day, both camps emerged thinking that they had gained what they were seeking. Arthur and the Stalwarts were certain that "pledges had been made," and that Garfield had promised cabinet positions, patronage power, and carte blanche in New York State in return for help in winning the election. In his own notes of the meeting, however, Garfield said that he was "very weary but . . . no mistakes had been made and probably much good had been done. No trades, no shackles."

The night of August 6, Garfield was treated to a rally in Madison Square Park lit by fifty thousand candles in the hands of supporters who had been assembled by Arthur and the city Republicans. Garfield spoke eloquently about the Civil War and commended those who had fought to end racial servitude. That was the public impression he left from his visit, but when Conkling appeared in New York hours after Garfield had departed, he scoffed that while Garfield might have taken the high road in his rhetoric, he had held out a cup to Arthur and Platt and, by extension, Conkling and "conceded anything and everything to the Stalwarts if they would only rush to the rescue and save the day."

And save the day they did. From his baronial suite in the Fifth Avenue Hotel, Arthur worked tirelessly on behalf of Garfield, levying assessments, raising money from donors, handling correspondence, wheedling and cajoling, wining and dining, getting speeches printed and distributed, organizing events, and, of course, collecting and doling out campaign funds. While firmly identified with the Stalwarts, Arthur managed to remain friendly with just about everyone who mattered. His ego, unlike Conkling's and Blaine's, did not walk into a room before he did, and few people felt strongly enough about him to hate him. He was the Teflon candidate of his day, and in an era of dirty campaigning, he neither received nor threw much mud.

On Arthur's urging, Senator Conkling eventually visited Garfield in Mentor to shake the candidate's hand. Fancifully dubbed the "Treaty of Mentor," the meeting temporarily placated Conkling, who then deigned to speak on behalf of the ticket. Ulysses S. Grant also made a campaign swing, for which he was well compensated. And for the pivotal state of Indiana, Arthur delegated Stephen Dorsey, the former carpetbag Arkansas senator. Dorsey was the ablest fund-raiser the Stalwarts had, though it was understood that he was a political operator not afraid to push beyond the limits of law and propriety. He was the type of political operative who gives politics a bad name. He was also remarkably effective at what he did.

Because the Democratic vice presidential nominee, William English, was from Indiana, the state was very much "in play." The Republicans were operating under the assumption that the Democrats would win the entire South and its 138 electoral votes. If the Democrats carried New York (where they were strong and organized), they would need only Indiana to put Hancock in the White House. Dorsey was dispatched because his skills were perfect for the task of delivering the state to the Republicans. Indiana had a rough-and-tumble reputation as a place where rules were rarely honored. Dorsey went to the land of the Hoosiers, got out some votes legally, and paid for others.

The result of these efforts was a narrow victory for Garfield and Arthur in November. More than 75 percent of eligible voters turned out on Election Day. Given that women were not enfranchised and recently emancipated blacks were being disenfranchised, that meant 9.2 million votes, of which 4,454,416 were cast for Garfield and 4,444,952 for Hancock. Third parties such as the Greenbacks received a few hundred thousand votes. Garfield's margin of victory was less than one-tenth of a percent, but the electoral college vote was not quite so close, at 214 to 155. The message was clear: the country in 1880, as in 1876 and again in 1884, was sharply and evenly divided, and the divisions were geographic. In 1880, not a single state south of the Mason-Dixon Line went Republican, and not a single state from the North went Democratic. Missouri and Kentucky both were won by the Democrats, but Indiana, California, Colorado, and Oregon all went Republican.

Though many have lamented the division between "red states" and "blue states" in the elections at the end of the twentieth century and into the twenty-first, the electoral map was just as starkly delineated in the 1870s and 1880s. In fact, the only real battlegrounds were New York and Indiana—New York because of Tammany Hall, Irish immigrants, and upstate urban machines in Buffalo and elsewhere that were cultivated by the Democrats; and Indiana because of populist rejection of both parties and because of peculiar electoral laws that made it easier for well-organized party officials to capture the state-wide delegation. Yet even though this generation still heard the echo of the Civil War, the solid Democratic South and nearly solid Republican North did not lead to cries of concern about the viability of the republic or the health of democracy.

Relieved to have eked out a victory, Garfield and Arthur celebrated, separately. They had won the ticket, but they lived hundreds of miles apart, barely knew each other, and were hardly friends. The inauguration wasn't until March 4, but from the day after the election, Garfield was busy fielding requests for appointments and Arthur was absorbed with getting Stalwarts into the cabinet. For Garfield, the key was to strike the right balance among Stalwarts, Half-Breeds, and other worthy claimants. After all, the Republicans had also won back control of the House of Representatives, and less prominent people who had contributed significantly to that outcome had to be rewarded. The *New York Times* wryly observed that so many factions were convinced that they had been promised cabinet positions that "if all reports are true, President Garfield's Cabinet will contain about one hundred and twenty-five persons."

The most crucial question was the balance of power between Blaine and Conkling, and it was soon evident that Blaine was the victor. He was asked to be secretary of state, a position then considered the second most important office in the nation, even though the diplomatic corps was small in size and the department had only a fraction of the appointments of the Treasury Department or the Post Office. Garfield flirted with placing Conkling in the cabinet as well, but Blaine vetoed the idea, saying that the New Yorker would be like "strychnine" to the Garfield administration, leading first "to contortions" and "then . . . death."

Arthur, meanwhile, basked in the cold of the New York winter and hosted dinner after dinner, one of which resulted in something of a tempest. A banquet was held by the Union League Club at Delmonico's to honor Stephen Dorsey for delivering Indiana to the Republicans. In a private room shrouded in dark wood, after hours of wine and rich food, with luminaries such as Henry Ward Beecher, John Jacob Astor, Jay Gould, and J. P. Morgan in attendance, toasts were made, including one by General Grant and another by Arthur himself, all of which were recorded by an enterprising reporter who attended the scene.

Though *Harper's Weekly* later described the evening as "queer," there was nothing odd about it. None have depicted the scene better than Arthur biographer Thomas Reeves. The dinner was a celebration of a naked bit of political chicanery. Dorsey had bullied and bought Indiana, and the result was victory. Dorsey thanked his compatriots and singled out Arthur for particular praise. "You have most of you known [Arthur] for a generation, but I can say he is the only candidate that I know of or ever heard of who during a national campaign had a private character and public record so thoroughly intrenched that they were alike unassailed and unassailable. . . . I have reason to believe that had it not been for his steady hand and clear head we would hardly be here tonight celebrating the victory of November last."

Such praise from a man widely regarded as "one of the most disreputable of the Arkansas carpetbaggers" might have been damning in itself, but Arthur proceeded to taste his own shoe leather. In his toast, he made several wink-and-nod allusions to moneys spent and deeds done, and then was overcome with a bout of coyness. "I don't think," he said drunkenly, "we had better go into the minute secrets of the campaign . . . because I see the reporters are present, who are taking it all down; and while there is no harm in talking about some things after the election is over you cannot tell what they may make of it, because the inauguration has not yet taken place . . . if I should get to going about the secrets of the campaign, there is no saying what I might say to make trouble between now and the 4th of March." He laughed about the rumor floated during the campaign that he had been born in Canada, not Vermont, and hence was ineligible for the presidency. He then said that Indiana was truly a Democrat state and that only through the, ahem, distribution "of tracts and political documents" had it been carried by the Republicans. He alluded to other tactics but didn't elaborate. "If it were not for the reporters," he announced, "I would tell you the truth."

Reform-minded editors like E. L. Godkin sighed that the episode confirmed the venality of politics, but the brunt of the criticism went toward Dorsey, not Arthur. Dorsey had already been the target of a congressional investigation into the "Star Route" scandals, a scheme that had made a number of Republican Party loyalists rich from postal route concessions at the federal government's expense. Though Arthur had been a host of the banquet honoring Dorsey, he was not centrally implicated in the subsequent firestorm, perhaps because he was liked but more likely because no one took him all that seriously.

Garfield and Arthur were sworn in on March 4, 1881, outside the Capitol by Chief Justice Morrison Waite. That evening, they were feted by thousands of guests at the inaugural ball at the Smithsonian. The Marine Band played Gilbert and Sullivan; the revelers ate turkey and oysters, danced, and admired a large statue of the Goddess of Liberty holding an electric light. The next day, Garfield and Arthur returned to the real world, one in which the fragile alliance keeping the Republican Party together was in imminent danger of falling apart.

The cabinet had been set after months of wrangling, and Conkling glumly recognized that Blaine had trumped him. Yes, Arthur was vice president, and in a Senate evenly divided between thirty-seven Republicans and thirty-seven Democrats, Arthur's vote would matter. (His friends had given him an ivory gavel so that he could perform his duties as president of the Senate with his accustomed aplomb.) But while the Senate was balanced, the cabinet was not. It contained only one major appointee allied with the Stalwarts, Thomas James, who had been made postmaster general. James, however, was a rarity—a Stalwart who was admired by the reformers. Other posts were filled by representatives of the Pennsylvania and Ohio Republican machines, and, in addition to James, Conkling had been temporarily mollified by the promise of friendly appointments for judgeships and for the all-important New York Customhouse.

For a brief few weeks, Garfield breathed easily. He thought he had satisfied the two most powerful and bitter factions. But he had not. The Stalwarts and the Half-Breeds remained locked in an obsessive duel. Blaine, from his perch as secretary of state, saw an opportunity to humiliate Conkling. He claimed that Garfield's willingness to endorse the Conkling nominees in New York was a slap in the face, and threatened to resign rather than bear the embarrassment. Although Blaine was just as histrionic and imperious as Conkling, he did not raise Garfield's hackles, and that gave him an advantage. On his urging, Garfield removed the collector of the New York Customhouse and nominated William Robertson to be the replacement. What made this doubly galling to Conkling was the fact that Robertson was a judge and a New York congressman who had betrayed Conkling and bolted to Blaine during the 1880 Republican convention.

Events moved swiftly. Robertson's name was submitted to the Senate on March 23, 1881, and Arthur as president of the Senate was one of the first to read it. He quickly informed Conkling, who was in the Senate chamber along with most of the senators because of a filibuster then being conducted by the Democrats against another slate of Garfield's nominees.

The drone of the filibuster was interrupted by a commotion near Conkling's desk as he and Arthur stared meaningfully at each other.

Soon, everyone knew what had happened. Conkling denounced Garfield for breaking his word and called the move "perfidy without parallel." Grant commented that Blaine had played Garfield so easily that it proved the president "lacked the backbone of an angle-worm." The *Nation* wrote that the whole imbroglio proved that nothing was going to change under Garfield. Robertson's nomination, the magazine commented, "was pure politics. . . . The causes are obscure but it is plain enough that improvement in the administration is not among the number." In his inaugural address only weeks before, Garfield had vowed to end one of the primary civil service abuses—"the arbitrary removal of officers." Yet there Garfield was, removing a perfectly adequate civil servant and replacing him for no other reason than politics.

Garfield reacted to the criticism with an appeal to high ideals. The issue, he claimed, "would settle the question of whether the President is registering clerk of the Senate or the Executive of the United States." He acted as if the nomination were one of principle, and not a pure power play, and he elevated the contest to one of balance of power between the branches of the government. Here, at least, he was onto something. The power of the president had been eroding ever since Lincoln was assassinated, and had migrated to brokers like Conkling and Blaine in government and to captains of industry outside of government. Garfield had been in the White House less than a month, and he had found that not only was the mansion in need of repair, but the entire office was in need of resuscitation. Said Whitelaw Reid, the editor of the *New York Tribune* and a Blaine confidant, the Robertson nomination "is the turning point of his whole Administration. . . . If Garfield surrenders now, Conkling is president for the rest of the term and Garfield becomes a laughing stock."

For his part, Conkling would have been no less offended had Garfield walked into the Senate chamber and spat in his face. He could not let the nomination go through. Arthur, though part of the administration, had little hesitation about choosing sides and lobbied for Conkling. After the Democratic filibuster ended in early May, the Robertson nomination was the top of the agenda. Sensing that public opinion was behind him, Garfield had stiffened and refused to withdraw the name. It was a battle for control, and Conkling quickly discovered that he lacked the votes to prevent the nomination. What he did next was astonishing.

He resigned.

Along with Senator Thomas Platt of New York, who would be known from then on as "Me Too Platt," Conkling quit the Senate. The plan was to be reelected resoundingly by the New York legislature, which would demonstrate that Garfield could not violate senatorial courtesy without consequences. The problem was that Conkling had lost touch with reality. Instead of sending tremors through Washington, Conkling's resignation was met with raised eyebrows, guffaws, and bemusement. "Lord Roscoe," said one senator, "was now the emperor without his clothes." Former president Hayes, in an interview with the *New York Herald*, said that Conkling was "a monomaniac on the subject of his own importance." The *New York Times* called the resignation "a blunder," and within weeks the once-friendly paper was questioning Conkling's future viability as a politician. No longer willing to do Conkling's bidding, the state legislature delayed the vote and then in late June decided not to return Conkling to the U.S. Senate.

Throughout this period, Arthur had rarely been far from Conkling's side, and many began to question his fitness to be vice president. He had been elected with Garfield, but he was acting as if he had been elected with Conkling. Said the *Nation*, "Vice-President Arthur's open and active conspiring with Conkling and Platt for their return to the Senate greatly heightens the indecency of the present situation." Not since John Calhoun defied Andrew Jackson during the nullification crisis of 1832, the paper continued, had a vice president so abused his office. In the space of two months, Arthur's political star had fallen precipitously. Roscoe Conkling, his patron, had made a historic gaffe; rarely has someone fallen out of power so quickly. Arthur had availed himself of Conkling's coattails for more than a decade, and he was tied to them as Conkling's career went into reverse.

Conkling had been accumulating enemies and adversaries for years, and like so many powerful men, he overreached. He forgot that people did his bidding not because they liked him but because he had power. Once that power was lost, he found that many of his friends were not so friendly. Arthur was a notable exception, but that speaks better of Arthur than of Conkling. Arthur remained loyal because he believed that it was the right thing to do and that Garfield had acted in a partisan and unfair fashion. Many other Stalwarts had had enough of Conkling's imperious ways and his overweening sense of himself, and they were no longer interested in fighting for him.

Conkling's self-immolation weakened Arthur's position in the administration. Blaine was triumphant, and Garfield was pleased that he had scored one for the executive branch. On July 2, 1881, Garfield and Blaine walked into the Baltimore and Potomac railroad station in Washington. Garfield was taking a trip to New York, and Blaine was seeing him off. But before Garfield had reached the platform, he was shot in the back. Quickly grabbed by onlookers and the police, the gunman, Charles Guiteau, calmly explained why he had just shot the president of the United States. "I did it and will go to jail for it. I am a Stalwart," he said, "and Arthur will be President."

Chester Arthur had stood by Conkling. Because of that, he was suddenly implicated in an assassination that would put him in the White House. Not the best way to become president, not the best way at all.

5

"Chet Arthur? President
of the United States? Good God!"

Chester Arthur was with Roscoe Conkling in New York City when word arrived by telegram that President Garfield had been shot. Arthur was understandably shaken by the news, and he quickly retired to the Fifth Avenue Hotel. Bits and pieces of information were trickling in, and it wasn't clear whether the president was still alive. The news that evening was not encouraging, and it was widely speculated that Garfield would not survive the night.

The following day, with the president's condition grave, Guiteau gave further statements to his jailers. He also had a letter with him when he was arrested that he had written in case he had been killed while committing the crime. It stated that "the President's tragic death was a sad necessity, but it will unite the Republican Party and save the Republic." Soon after, another letter was found in his apartment addressed to "President Arthur," which contained Guiteau's suggestions for the composition of the new cabinet.

The uncertainty of whether Garfield would live or die, combined with the emerging picture of an assassin who claimed to be acting on the Stalwarts' behalf, placed Arthur in an unenviable position. He had to allay suspicion that he was in any way associated with Guiteau, and he could not do anything to suggest that he was eager to assume Garfield's place. Initially, he was so concerned that the slightest misstep on his part could be misinterpreted that he didn't want to go to Washington at all. Safer to stay out of sight in his New York home than venture into the glare of the public spotlight and get burned. But, speaking for the cabinet, Blaine asked that Arthur come to the capital and reassure a nervous public that the government was intact. Arthur left New York immediately, and the overnight train deposited him in Washington the morning of July 4.

Personally, Arthur appeared devastated. Observers noted that the vice president's eyes were bloodshot and frequently welled with tears. He offered to stay with Mrs. Garfield by the president's bed, but that was not considered appropriate. Meanwhile, people suddenly realized that Arthur might become president, something almost no one had anticipated or desired, including Arthur himself. Even his onetime allies found the prospect disturbing. "Gen. Arthur," wrote the *New York Times*, "has held for four months an office which acquires importance only in view of such an emergency as the crime of Guiteau was intended to create. . . . Active politicians, uncompromising partisans, have held before now the office of Vice-President of the United States, but no holder of that office has ever made it so plainly subordinate to his self-interest as a politician and narrowness as a partisan." The paper lamented that in the weeks before the assassination attempt, Arthur had squandered reservoirs of goodwill and had justified the fears of his detractors. As a result, the paper, which had supported Arthur throughout the customhouse battle with

Hayes and during the campaign of 1880, concluded that as far as the presidency was concerned, "Gen. Arthur is about the last man who would be considered eligible to that position." Trying to find some saving grace, *Harper's* commented that in the future, nominating conventions would take the choice of vice president more seriously. If the price for better choices in the future was a Chester Arthur administration, well, perhaps that was worth it.

Arthur himself remained quietly in Washington for several weeks while Garfield was operated on by a team of physicians. They were unable to locate the bullet that had lodged near his spleen, but the president seemed to rally in mid-July. The worst seemed to have passed, and Arthur returned to Manhattan. But soon Garfield began to slip. He could not eat, and his wounds were infected by the repeated careless probing of his doctors. By late August, it was clear that Garfield would not survive the end of summer.

By September 1, the president's physicians concluded that it was only a matter of weeks. Garfield had been moved to the New Jersey shore to get some relief from the humid cauldron of Washington, and Arthur was told to prepare for the worst. A few snippets about Arthur's mood were recorded by friends who talked with him during this period. The normally ebullient New Yorker was subdued and shaken. Given the whispering and wondering about shadowy connections between the president's assailant and Arthur's faction, Arthur viewed becoming president as a "calamity."

Garfield died the evening of September 19. He had all but wasted away by then and weighed barely 120 pounds. Relaxed to be near the sea, Garfield developed a fever and could not fight the infection. Arthur was informed of the president's passing just before midnight. After sobbing alone in his library, he wired the attorney general expressing his sorrow and offering Mrs. Garfield his sympathy. In New York, crowds gathered in front of city hall and in Madison Square Park near Arthur's Lexington Avenue home. They called for him, but he remained inside, surrounded by friends, including Elihu Root (who was then at the beginning of a long and illustrious career in government). The transition of power was brief and joyless. Arthur was administered the oath of office by a state judge and was sworn in as the nation's twenty-first president at 2:15 on the morning of September 20, 1881.

Though Garfield was the second president to be shot in the space of sixteen years, the public mood during these twilight months was remarkably calm. Politics did not cease, but most major issues were held in limbo. One exception was the final defeat of Conkling in the New York legislature, after the former senator attempted one more procedural gambit to get himself reelected. Washington in July and August has never been an active time, and Garfield's precarious health only added to the lethargy. But while political activity slowed nearly to a halt, the country was not exactly grief stricken. Yes, people were pensive and sad and alarmed, but the stakes seemed less high than they had been when Lincoln was shot or than they would be when McKinley and later Kennedy were killed. There was little hand-wringing about the fate of the nation, and there were few jeremiads. Garfield had not touched a chord. His personality was too moderate and the office of the presidency too hobbled. And his assassin turned out to be less than initially supposed.

Guiteau was not, as news accounts labeled him, a disgruntled office seeker, except in his own mind. He had been floating around Washington and New York for years trying to catch the favor of the powers that were. In an era when there were fewer gatekeepers separating men of influence from those who wanted to meet them, Guiteau had wandered into Senate offices and White House anterooms seeking audiences, and he had written a steady stream of letters to dozens of congressmen and federal officials. He imagined himself a loyal Republican who had been repeatedly denied a post because of factional maneuvers between Stalwarts and Half-Breeds, and he believed that killing Garfield would remove that logjam. In the days after the shooting, there was legitimate concern that Guiteau was linked to the Stalwarts and that the attempt on the president's life would give rise to a political crisis. Once the investigators realized that Guiteau was acting alone and that his connection to external reality was tenuous, that concern abated.

Garfield's prolonged struggle to live also dissipated some of the tension. Rather than one shocking moment, Garfield's assassination lasted two and a half months. One week he seemed to be improving, the next not, and after two months there was a natural tendency for the public to become more detached. By the time Garfield died, most Americans were already prepared for it.

But one man, at least, was not. Arthur had tried to banish all thoughts of becoming president until the very end. Insofar as he could, he kept to himself in those first days. The nature of an Arthur administration had been the subject of feverish speculation in elite circles, and now that he was actually president, a number of skeptics decided to give him the benefit of the doubt. The *New York Times*, fresh from its attacks on Arthur's character, ran a lengthy interview with an ex-governor praising Arthur as "a hard-money man, in favor of a proper protection of American industries, a friend of the working class . . . and able, upright, honorable, and efficient." The next day the paper recanted further and declared that although Arthur had fumbled during the spring in showing favoritism to Conkling, he remained "a warm-hearted, impulsive man." To allay fears, the *Times* advised President Arthur to "know principles rather than individuals, [to] subordinate personal preferences as well as acquired prejudices to the accomplishment of certain well-defined public ends." All in all, however, the paper judged Arthur to be "a much better and broader man than the majority of those with whom his recent career has been identified."

Arthur went directly to Elberon, New Jersey, where Garfield had spent his final weeks, to escort the funeral party to Washington. The ceremony in the capital was somber and beautiful. The procession rolled down Pennsylvania Avenue as tens of thousands of mourners lined the way. The coffin was placed in the Capitol rotunda, where it remained for a day before the body was taken back to Cleveland for burial. In the meantime, Arthur again took the oath of office, administered by Chief Justice Waite, and he delivered an inaugural address. "Men may die," President Arthur intoned, "but the fabrics of our free institutions remain unshaken. No higher or more assuring proof could exist of the strength and permanence of popular government than the fact that though the chosen of the people be struck down his constitutional successor is peacefully installed without shock or strain except the sorrow which mourns the bereavement." He then gave thanks that in this time of grief and stress, no issue demanded immediate resolution, and no threats imperiled the country. "Summoned to these high duties and responsibilities and profoundly conscious of their magnitude and gravity, I assume the trust imposed by the Constitution, relying for aid on divine guidance and the virtue, patriotism and intelligence of the American people."

No one knew what direction the Arthur administration would take, not even Arthur himself. The only certainty was that most of the cabinet would be replaced. A president's cabinet was seen as an extension of his personal patronage, and no one expected Garfield's appointees to remain in their posts long. As to Arthur's agenda, that was opaque, but Garfield's had not exactly been clear and pointed. While people were curious about what Arthur would focus on, he did not have to deal with unfavorable comparisons with his predecessor. Garfield had been in office for only four months before the shooting, and his time had been almost entirely consumed with managing the politics of appointments, which had culminated with the standoff with Conkling. Unlike most vice presidents who have abruptly become president, Arthur could steer just about any course he chose.

Few would deny that there was something odd and unsettling about Arthur becoming chief executive. Even with the decline of presidential prestige in the 1870s, most people, consciously or not, had a vestigial awe for the office. Americans wanted to believe that the president was at worst first among equals. There had been some disappointments in the past— most recently Andrew Johnson—but almost all the prior occupants had commanded authority or elicited strong passions. But Arthur was different. He had not been elected to any office prior to the vice presidency, and he had never been seen as a leader. Conkling, Blaine, Grant, and dozens of other names came before his in the hierarchy of the 1870s, and juxtaposed to dynamic industrialists like Morgan, Gould, Carnegie, and Rockefeller, Arthur's star appeared dimmer yet. He was respected and respectable. Save for his miscue in the spring of 1881 he had earned a reputation for integrity in a system known for corruption. But that didn't make him presidential, yet there he was, the president of the United States.

That had happened less because of Arthur's skills and ambition than because he was acceptable. Often, it isn't the ones who are best suited who rise to prominence but the ones who make the fewest enemies. Arthur never attracted the passionate allegiance that Blaine or Conkling did, but he avoided the passionate animosity they engendered. Much like Garfield, Arthur rose in 1880 because he was still standing. He was never the tallest reed, and so he was rarely knocked down. Though he was a skilled organizer and a more-than-competent politico, he lacked the x factor usually associated with leadership and greatness. As it turned out, the qualities he did possess allowed him to rise farther than many others who were more intelligent, dynamic, and driven. When he ascended to the highest office in the country, he was able to use those qualities to govern more successfully than many had expected.

For someone so identified with partisan politics, Arthur himself was remarkably equitable and nonpartisan. He had a strong sense of fair play, and he did not have an exaggerated sense of self. He respected that other people of other parties and factions held strong beliefs and desires, and in the interests of order and national unity he intended to construct an inclusive administration. He seems to have come to that conclusion automatically, and it dictated his response to Conkling and the Stalwarts when they turned to him in October and expected an open door and a warm embrace.

It had not yet dawned on Conkling that his day had passed. He fully expected to be offered one of the two or three most important cabinet posts, and he preferred the Treasury. He also assumed that once Blaine had resigned, Arthur would remove Robertson from the New York Customhouse and install a Stalwart. Arthur, however, had other ideas. He met with Conkling for an hour in late October, and although Conkling emerged from the White House with a jaunty grin, there was something forced about his expression. It soon became apparent that Arthur had said no to Conkling's demands. It would be bad for the country, and lethal for Arthur's credibility, if the first thing he did as president was staff the executive branch with cronies. Whatever debt Arthur may have owed Conkling personally, he knew that it would be political suicide to be seen as Lord Roscoe's puppet. But the refusal was more than tactical. The assassination of Garfield had placed the issue of civil service reform at the center of the national agenda, and one of the tenets of reform was that naked favoritism should not dictate appointments.

Arthur, however, sent mixed signals. While keeping the Stalwarts at arm's length, he did use his new patronage powers to cement an alliance with William Mahone of Virginia. As one of two independents in a Senate with thirty-seven Republicans and thirty-seven Democrats, Mahone was wooed by both parties. His price was influence, and though Garfield had been unwilling to pay it in the spring, Arthur, who had been closer to the goings-on in the Senate, conceded in order to gain Mahone's vote for the Republicans. That did not impress the reformers, who concluded that Arthur would soon revert to the spoils system that had succored him. As Garfield's cabinet began to resign, those fears increased. "The new administration," wrote the now perpetually irate Henry Adams, "will be the center for every element of corruption, south and north. The outlook is very discouraging."

Faced with a new president whose grace and modesty stymied his critics, Adams declared that it would be hard for the reformers to make any inroads. The fight would be lonely, and Adams was discouraged, save for one thing: Blaine announced his resignation. That alone gave Adams some comfort. Blaine symbolized the spoils system, and his departure combined with Conkling's was a small victory. Adams, however, was by nature indisposed to see any cup as more than half full. "Like all the rest of the world," he wrote Henry Cabot Lodge, "I am throwing up my cap for Mr. Arthur, whose social charms we now understand to be most extraordinary, although only last spring we were assured by the same people that he was a vulgar and dull animal. To be in fashion is the first law of nature. My mouth is shut on reform politics for at least two years to come. I have not the physical strength to cry like St. John in the wilderness."

Blaine had tendered his resignation even though he harbored none of the animus for Arthur personally that he did for Conkling. He just could not see himself serving under a Stalwart president and chose instead to bide his time until the next election in 1884. Arthur appointed a former senator from New Jersey, Frederick Frelinghuysen, to succeed Blaine as secretary of state. He also replaced Attorney General William MacVeagh with Benjamin Brewster of Pennsylvania, and he appointed Charles Folger of New York as secretary of the Treasury. Arthur did retain one of Garfield's appointees: Robert Todd Lincoln, the only surviving son of Abraham Lincoln. Arthur asked Lincoln to stay on as secretary of war, and Lincoln remained in office until the end of Arthur's term. All of these men were highly regarded by party loyalists and by reformers. They had assembled résumés based primarily on talent rather than on their connections, and they served as a reminder that even in this era some politicians were genuinely dedicated to public service. Not all of Arthur's appointments were honorable, at least not in the eyes of the reformers, but it was a pleasant surprise to see the new president assemble a cabinet that did not raise hackles.

Like any new chief executive, Arthur was inundated with patronage requests. He could easily have spent all his working and social hours interviewing candidates for the thousands of jobs at his disposal. He wisely limited time spent on appointments and interviews to three days a week (Monday, Wednesday, and Thursday), and he delegated department heads to use their discretion as long as they were guided by notions of fairness and not simply faction. Arthur also began to grate at the seeming familiarity that many of these petitioners assumed. One group of delegates strode into his office, put their feet up on his desk, and called him "Chet." He curtly instructed them that he was now president, that they should remove their feet or be removed from the office, and that they should address him as "Mr. President."

Arthur was a nice man, but he had his pride. That may have been one reason for refusing Conkling and allowing Blaine to depart. He did not want to be seen as anyone's errand boy. At other stages and in other roles, whether as quartermaster or collector, he hadn't minded being seen as a Stalwart following someone else's lead because that was appropriate given his position. But the president was not supposed to be a follower, and to be effective the person occupying the office had to be seen as autonomous and independent. Arthur had always tried to do his job as well as possible. In previous roles, that demanded loyalty and sublimation of his own views to the will of others. In this new role, it meant bowing to no one and refusing to let others treat him as he had been treated in the past.

His new demeanor was on display when he delivered his first message to Congress on December 6, 1881. It was a measured, sophisticated address, demonstrating an impressive grasp of domestic and international affairs. That was a surprise. Arthur had spent most of his life immersed in politics, and though the term *inside the Beltway* did not yet exist, the principle was the same. Those who wrote about politics and those involved in politics in these years often invested petty battles over influence and patronage with mythopoetic significance. Meanwhile, millions of Americans went about their lives unconcerned about whether a New York Stalwart or a Pennsylvania Half-Breed got the job of assistant postmaster general. They had lives that were barely touched by Washington, and absent the questions of slavery and national identity that had flared in the 1850s, they cared only intermittently about what went on in the nation's capital.

Arthur's address, however, spoke both to the political class and to the American public. Whether or not he wrote the entire address (though he certainly wrote some of it—in this era, the White House did not employ a staff of speechwriters), he discussed everything from the recent death of Garfield, to the composition of the civil service and the need for reform, to foreign relations, Indian wars, the economy, and the settling of the West.

He began by acknowledging the tragedy of the assassination, yet he quickly reminded Congress that it had been a prosperous year and, with the exception of Guiteau's violent assault, a calm one. The United States had seen an outpouring of international sympathy after Garfield lost his struggle against death. Though

he did not mention Blaine by name, he lauded the former secretary of state for his assiduous work cultivating better relations with the states of Central and South America, where
U.S. businesses were beginning to find ample opportunities. He
was happy to report that in 1881 the U.S. government took in
$360 million and had only $260 million in expenditures, of
which the largest amount ($80 million) was for interest on the
debt that the government was still paying off from the Civil
War. Customs duties accounted for $200 million of govern-
ment revenue, postal services for another $36 million. The pop-
ulation had grown from 30 million in 1860 to 50 million in the
census of 1880, and, given the surplus and the still-rising cus-
tom revenues, Arthur proposed the abolition of all "internal
revenue taxes except those upon tobacco . . . and upon dis-
tilled spirits and fermented liquors." He called for a revision of
the tariff laws and for the maintenance of the army at its current level of thirty thousand enlisted men, most deployed in
fighting Indian tribes in the West and Southwest.

Arthur devoted considerable attention to Indian affairs.
The formidable adversary Sitting Bull had finally surrendered,
and now the federal government had to turn to the issue of
settlement on reservations and organizing territorial governments. The only other question that Arthur dwelt on at such
length was civil service reform. Arthur reminded Congress of
his message as vice president endorsing reform, but he now
went further and spoke approvingly of English civil service
laws. The English professional civil service provided job tenure
and pension guarantees. These features made it possible for
England to attract young men to the civil service with the
promise of many years of employment and sufficient income.
That allowed civil servants to focus on serving the public good,
rather than on their own job security. And to ensure that the

best candidates were selected, there was a civil service exam as a filter. Arthur concluded that while not all elements of the English system could be adopted, he was in favor of some version of it for the United States.

This was a dramatic departure from the stalemate on civil service reform, and it was a direct result of Guiteau and the Garfield assassination. Guiteau had gone on trial in November, and though he was deemed an unhinged loner, his words the day he shot Garfield acted as a catalyst to reform. The fact that Arthur now chose to lead reform rather than obstruct it tipped the balance permanently.

Observers from across the political spectrum were impressed with his first weeks. Reformers had been burned too often and were wary of presidential rhetoric, yet they cautiously applauded Arthur's seeming conversion. Others appreciated the knowledge and maturity that Arthur exhibited in his message to Congress. All in all, the year ended well for the former Gentleman Boss. But, warned the *Nation*'s E. L. Godkin, "every administration has a honeymoon. . . . That is largely owing to the good nature of the American people, as well as to the honorable desire of every just man that those who have a difficult task before them should have a fair chance and a pleasant start." Come the new year, the bar would be raised. Arthur had "the advantage of doing better than his opponents predicted he would do. . . . But the credit thus gained has induced his friends to indulge in glowing predictions as to his future achievements, and consequently the standard will now be much higher and far more difficult to reach."

In short, it was easy to talk of civil service reform, a prosperous country, and its expansion. Would Arthur be able to turn honeyed words into action? Many people hoped so; most of them doubted it.

6

A New House and an
Eventful Year

At the beginning of 1882, at least one thing was certain: the White House was a mess. Its past two residents had both complained about the dowdy decoration and a persistent draftiness. Mrs. Lucy Hayes had made some alterations to the decor, but "Lemonade Lucy" also banned the consumption of alcohol, which did not endear her to Chester Arthur. It was rumored that one of the first things Arthur said when he became president was "I will not live in that house," and true to his word, he waited three months before moving in, both to give Mrs. Garfield time to move out and to do some emergency redecorating. When he moved into the executive mansion in December 1881, Arthur brought his younger sister, Mary McElroy, as a proxy first lady, and the White House was soon engulfed in a flurry of renovation.

In addition to taking over the primary care of Arthur's ten-year-old daughter, Ellen, Mary oversaw an extensive remodeling of the White House interiors. Arthur's homes in New York City had been marked by their opulence and panache, and he wanted the White House to reflect that sensibility. That inclination was not without controversy. Ever since the presidential mansion was burned by the British during the War of 1812, Americans have vested the White House with a certain amount of symbolism. The decorative perambulations of chief executives and their wives not only marked but often determined the style and tone for the houses of the rich and powerful throughout the country. Given that the aesthetic and culinary choices could not possibly have satisfied all sensibilities, the decisions were usually met with a mix of celebration and sniping.

Arthur, however, didn't hesitate to order a thorough remodeling. And while he was assessing architectural plans, he also worked with Mary to replace the dowdy menus of Hayes and Garfield with something more akin to the offerings at Delmonico's. He hired a French chef from New York to create state dinners, and he installed the personal cook who had been with him for years. The interior redesign of the mansion would take months, if not longer, but in the meantime there was still dinner and drinks to consider. Widower though he was, Arthur preferred to spend his nights dining with the same type of companions that he had during his years of prominence and prosperity in New York. He had not been a workaholic then, and he did not become one as president. Evenings were open to quiet diversions or elaborate entertainment and, under his aegis, the White House became a social destination in a capital not known for social destinations.

But the furnishings just had to go. Arthur cleared out wagonloads of furniture, which were then sold and auctioned off. At the time, few Americans gave much thought to preserving legacies for history. The new was worshipped, the old usually cast aside. To the dismay of archivists and preservationists, the White House of the nineteenth century was a revolving door of styles and motifs, and successive occupants discarded past desiderata with little consideration for the desires of future generations for artifacts. Gilded Age mansions throughout the country were built at great cost and with the best artistry of the day, and then torn down ten or twenty years later to make way for new ones. The White House, because it had become a monument of American power and liberty, couldn't be torn down, but it could be torn apart and redone.

For that task, Arthur chose Louis Comfort Tiffany, a thirty-three-year-old former landscape painter whose firm, Associated Artists, was just beginning to carve out a reputation for daring approaches to design that went beyond the overstuffed ecstasies of the Victorian era. Tiffany had grand dreams of changing the way Americans saw beauty, and he was starting to put those ideas into practice. Instead of heavy drapery and sturdy, stuffed furniture, he envisioned light and glass. Though Arthur had been quite comfortable with the Victorian fashions of the 1860s and 1870s, he had always been what today we would call "fashion forward," and he gave Tiffany carte blanche. The result was a new entrance and a Blue Room that lived up to its name.

Tiffany was not yet famous for his lamps, but in 1881 he obtained a patent for a new technique to decorate stained glass. In the Cross Hall of the White House, he installed a large stained-glass screen, which inspired one magazine to rhapsodize that the only dark things left in the White House were the oil portraits of former presidents. The Blue Room itself was painted, not surprisingly, a light sky blue, and the ceiling was decorated with painted stars. Tiffany and his workers also painstakingly applied wallpaper inlaid with pieces of sparkling glass. Other parts of the mansion were similarly redone. The

Red Room became more strikingly red; Arthur's office gained a more open fireplace and yellow tones; and gold leaf appeared promiscuously throughout the public rooms. The executive mansion also acquired its first elevator.

Combined with the emphasis on grand meals, elaborate table settings, and entertainment, the Arthur White House easily surpassed its predecessors. It may be, as future occupant John F. Kennedy quipped, that the executive mansion was never filled with more intellectual brilliance than when Thomas Jefferson dined alone. By the same token, it was rarely filled with such hedonistic grace as when Chester Arthur hosted a dinner party. In that respect, Arthur is unsurpassed. Twenty years later, Theodore Roosevelt removed the Tiffany glass screen and redid the decor. Roosevelt had his own ideas of how to live, and he unceremoniously erased Arthur's traces, just as his were erased by later twentieth-century presidents who wanted the mansion to reflect their times.

There was one other fashion statement that caught attention: Chester Arthur's carriage. In an era before automobiles and secret service caravans, the presidential carriage was taken as a symbol of the administration. In that respect, it was like a mini–White House. There wasn't much to do in Washington, and speculation and gossip about a new president's primary form of public locomotion could fill a number of otherwise dreary evenings. Arthur took several months to unveil his horse-drawn conveyance, but when he did, everyone understood why he had been dubbed the Gentleman Boss.

"It is no exaggeration to say that it is the finest which has ever appeared in the streets of the capital," gurgled the *New York Times*. "The carriage, from the New York Broome Street Brewsters, is a landau of novel design, painted a dark, mellow green, relieved with enough picking out in red to show the outline without being conspicuous. The trimmings are of morocco and cloth, the cushions and doors being faced with heavy lace. . . . The inside of the carriage is Labrador otter, beautifully lined with dark green and having the monogram C.A.A. worked in silk. The horses, two in number, are magnificent animals—mahogany bays with black points and without a white spot anywhere. . . . The entire turn-out is a model of quiet magnificence and good taste." The Brewsters, makers of the carriage, must have been delighted. In the Gilded Age, Chester Arthur was the closest thing to Jacqueline Kennedy that Washington would see until Jacqueline Kennedy. He set trends for stylish living emulated by thousands who could afford it and envied by millions who could not.

Having settled in the White House, Arthur soon established a work rhythm. As in his New York days, he kept his hours short, rarely longer than nine to five, beginning with a light breakfast and then followed by meetings with callers who ranged from congressmen to tourists. He was always perfectly attired, but visitors were equally struck by how polite he was. He tried to go for a ride or a stroll each day. He dined at seven when it was just family, and later when he was entertaining. On nights when he wasn't, he read government reports or dipped into his favorite authors, who included Thackeray and Dickens.

At the beginning of 1882, after four months as president, Arthur still had hundreds of vacancies to fill. Congress was preparing to pass several controversial bills, and dormant civil service legislation was now on the front burner. Arthur continued to court Senator Mahone of Virginia in an attempt to give the Republicans a narrow advantage in an evenly divided

Senate, and that aroused controversy within the party. The wounds from the Civil War had healed, but only with scar tissue. Mahone aroused fury among the Democrats, who treated him as a traitor, and resentment among the Republicans, who were stung by the favoritism shown to him by Garfield and now by Arthur. First, Mahone had gotten the federal government to relieve, or adjust, some of Virginia's debt burden (hence the name of his followers, "the Readjusters"), and now he was becoming a power in the national party. To many, Mahone looked like a carpetbagger in reverse, but for Arthur, placating him was simply good politics and gave both his nascent administration and the Republican Party an advantage.

With vacancies came advice on how to fill them, from illustrious leaders of the party such as Ulysses Grant and even from Conkling. Arthur wanted to reward his former patron and offered to nominate Conkling to the Supreme Court that spring. Conkling, deeming it better to rule in private practice than to serve on the bench, refused; there were no further overtures. Grant seems to have overstayed his welcome, and while he was one of the first honored guests at Arthur's table, the president began to resent the barrage of unsolicited advice that Grant delivered.

A banquet for Grant on March 22 was reported with delight by the journalistic corps, who themselves enjoyed the festivities along with the general and his wife. Secretary of State Frelinghuysen was there, along with numerous senators and representatives, and the dining room was decorated with azalea trees and roses. A few people sniped that Arthur's competence as a host was not matched by his abilities as chief executive, but they enjoyed the libations all the same. Arthur, who preferred to keep politics off the dinner table, steered clear of explicit discussions with Grant about the shape of the administration, and their interaction from then on was polite but often strained.

The following year, Grant's financial fortunes, which had been deteriorating at a relentless pace, worsened even more. A bill was introduced in Congress to give Grant the rank and salary of an active general. Arthur would not support the measure. He made the case that only the president had the authority to appoint generals and that allowing Congress to do so would set a dangerous precedent that would weaken the executive. Grant, understandably, didn't believe that logic, and was bitterly offended.

Arthur had gone further than most had supposed possible in distancing himself from the Stalwarts. Having established his independence and authority, he then quietly began to make secondary and tertiary appointments that rewarded his friends and allies, many of whom were in fact old Stalwarts. But by keeping aloof from Grant, Conkling, and the most powerful members of that faction and by fashioning a balanced and competent cabinet, Arthur avoided what would have been a crushing liability. Had he acted in a way to feed suspicions that he was simply a spoilsman, his entire term would have been reduced to the status of a lame duck, and it would have been an unpleasant few years. Arthur was a political enough animal to respect the law of first impressions, and as president he made few false moves in his first six months. And having established a grudging respect, he then confronted Congress over a popular, and odious, bill.

California in the 1880s was no longer the frontier territory of prospectors and forty-niners, but it was still a land of opportunity that drew people from across the continent and around the world. The transcontinental railroad was completed at Utah's Promontory Point in 1869 and then upgraded in the 1870s. It linked California to the eastern and central United States. As a result, California's cities blossomed, and its farms began to produce a cornucopia of agricultural goods. Then as now, however, much of the hard, physical work needed to construct this idyll was done by immigrants, and then as now, those immigrants had a rude welcome.

When Arthur became president, there were approximately 250,000 Chinese living in the United States, with the overwhelming majority in California. Few were citizens, and the Naturalization Act of 1870 made it impossible for them (or anyone else who wasn't either white or of African descent) to obtain citizenship. Chinese laborers, first brought to the United States as "coolies" whose legal status was in a netherworld between indentured servants and slaves, had built the railroads and then harvested crops. They were domestic servants and laborers in cities from Stockton to Sacramento. They were grudgingly admired for their fortitude, discipline, and work ethic, and for the same reasons, they were feared and reviled. They were, in short, too good at what they did. They did what others could do, but they worked harder and were paid less. Soon enough, in the divide-and-conquer logic of nativist politicians, they became the target of riots, and lynchings, and then, finally, of laws meant to prevent them from competing for the expanding pie of economic rewards.

The United States may be a country of immigrants, but rarely has a generation gone by without some furor over immigration. The uproar over the Chinese in the 1880s was simply the anti-immigration issue du jour. When New England attracted non-Puritan settlers in the later part of the seventeenth century, worried villagers passed laws to keep them out.

When 1.5 million Irish Catholics fled from famine to Boston and New York in the 1840s and early 1850s, they were the object of derision, prejudice, and hatred. They were caricatured as agents of the pope, as unwashed and unschooled, and as an unwelcome foreign presence whose major contributions to American life were loose morals and liquor. In time, these prejudices faded, and the Irish established themselves as civic leaders and powerful voting blocs. The Irish experience suggests that while the animus against the Chinese in the West had a strong racial component, racism alone wasn't the cause of the backlash. The United States may have been seen as a land of opportunity and possibility, but few Americans at any given time felt secure. Each wave of immigration was seen by some as a clear and present threat. In an already competitive economy, new immigrants meant new workers who would do whatever needed doing and for less money.

The harsh economy of the 1870s also stoked resentment. A quarter to half of the U.S. labor force was looking for work. Unemployed men gathered in taverns and public squares. They wanted jobs, and they wanted explanations for why they didn't have them. Many politicians obliged. It was easy to put the blame on strange foreigners who could not vote and who were at the mercy of the law. Anti-Chinese sentiment became a proxy for class war. Chinese immigration was the product of the insatiable demand of railroad companies, such as the Central Pacific, for cheap labor that could be forced to work and even to die without arousing the ire of do-good reformers. Ironically, some of the most virulent opponents of Chinese immigration were the Irish, who had only recently gained a measure of acceptance in mainstream America. Dennis Kearney of San Francisco made his political career rallying out-of-work laborers around the slogan "The Chinese must go." There was a logic to his animosity. One of the best ways to deflect attention is to find a common adversary, and by shifting blame to Chinese immigrants, Kearney was able to make common cause with people who might otherwise have targeted him. Kearney was hardly the first or last American politician to adopt such tactics.

In 1882, anti-Chinese sentiment in the West reached a fever pitch. John Miller, a Republican senator from California, called for a law to exclude Chinese immigrants for the next twenty years. The measure had widespread, bipartisan support not just in California but throughout the country. Labor groups in the Northeast treated all new immigrants as a danger to stable wages, and anti-immigration bills had been a good way to stir up voters. If it wasn't the Irish in the 1840s, it was the Chinese in the 1880s. The bill, called the Anti-Chinese Immigration Bill and later dubbed the Chinese Exclusion Act, swiftly made its way through Congress and in early spring was deposited on Chester Arthur's desk for his signature. To the astonishment and outrage of many in Congress, the president vetoed it.

The reason he gave was that the twenty-year exclusion violated treaty arrangements between the Chinese emperor and the U.S. government. Arthur claimed that the new bill would be seen by the Chinese government as a bad-faith gesture, and that it was his duty as chief executive to temper the hasty instincts of Congress and preserve the diplomatic credibility of the United States. The liberal press applauded the veto and saluted Arthur for standing on principle even in the face of popular demagoguery. In his veto message, Arthur objected to the bill's requirement that Chinese immigrants already in America be required to register, as if their activities needed monitoring by the government. He lauded the constructive role that Chinese labor had played in the expansion of the country and the construction of the railroads. The bill, he said, would backfire and hurt the American economy. Exclusion laws, he warned, would "repel Oriental nations from us and . . . drive their trade and commerce into more friendly hands."

Congress failed to overturn the veto, but Arthur did not win many friends in California by his actions. Popular opinion tilted in favor of a bill, and Arthur, who had rarely been a galvanizing figure on any side of any issue, found himself at the center of a maelstrom. He was burned in effigy in cities and towns in the West, and a new bill was quickly drafted that lowered the exclusion period from twenty years to ten. E. L. Godkin was not alone in lambasting the Republicans. A party that had been created by Lincoln and many others to fight the injustice of racial slavery was now championing a measure designed to bar a racial group from the country and prevent those already living in the United States from enjoying rights as citizens. But Republican politicians pressed ahead, unconcerned about such hypocrisy and untroubled by the moral contradictions.

When the new bill was submitted to Arthur, he knew that there were enough votes in Congress to overturn his veto and that public opinion, manipulated by demagogues, was eager to have the Chinese barred. Another president might have vetoed the bill again and forced Congress to overturn him. Clearly, Arthur's sympathies lay in that direction. He had been raised by a father with strong religious convictions against slavery, and he himself had been squarely in the antislavery camp as a young adult in the 1850s. In that sense, he was a true Republican in the mold of Lincoln and the founders of the party. At the same time, his political career was not built on the passion of his ideals; it had been based on his loyalty, diligence, and effectiveness as an operator. He was never a demagogue, and one reason why he had made so few enemies was that he was rarely petty, venal, or hateful. The Chinese exclusion bill was all three, but Arthur would not fight a fight he knew he would lose. Rather than be a martyr to principle, he submitted to the will of the political majority and pragmatically signed the ten-year exclusion act.

This legislative frenzy was soon followed by a frenzy of another sort. During the previous months, the trial of Charles Guiteau had been covered obsessively by the press. It was one of several high-profile trials of the Gilded Age, and it generated hyperbolic commentary. While the focus on Guiteau was understandable given the magnitude of his offense, the actual case was so simple that it required real effort to make it dramatic. The facts were never in doubt: Guiteau had walked into the train station on July 2, shot the president, declared his guilt, and was arrested with his weapon in hand. That should have made the trial brief to nonexistent save for the fact that Guiteau's lawyers decided to argue what was then a novel and untested defense. Their client, they claimed, was insane and not criminally liable for his actions.

Guiteau, it must be admitted, acted oddly from the moment he was arrested. He spent his time in prison composing the lecture series he planned to give once he was released. He expressed confidence that Arthur would help him. He gave frequent interviews and entertained hundreds of callers, many of them women, who wanted to see this assassin for themselves. His bizarre optimism about his future, along with his vituperative animosity toward his own legal team, bemused and delighted reporters. At his arraignment in Washington, Guiteau announced: "I plead not guilty to the indictment and my defense is threefold: 1. Insanity, in that it was God's act and not mine. The Divine pressure on me to remove the president was so enormous that it destroyed my free agency, and therefore I am not legally responsible for my act. 2. The president died from malpractice . . . if he had been well treated he would have recovered. 3. The president died in New Jersey, and, therefore, beyond the jurisdiction of this court." This was beyond outlandish, and it made very, very good copy for newspapers eager for a story to garner readers.

The trial lasted for most of December and January. The defense attempted to convince a skeptical jury that Guiteau was too addled to bear responsibility for his actions. Guiteau struck almost everyone as vainglorious and strange, but certainly not so insane that he deserved to be released from criminal culpability for killing the president of the United States. Whatever was meant by the term *insane*, and there was considerable confusion, few believed that Guiteau was not fully aware of his actions. On January 23, 1882, to Guiteau's evident surprise, the jury took all of an hour to sentence him to death.

Almost six months later, on the morning of June 30, Guiteau sat in his cell in Washington. Before making his way to the gallows, he composed a poem titled "I Am Going to the Lordy." Thousands turned out to witness his hanging, and it was, for a moment, a medieval scene of shouting, hooting, cursing, and booing. Guiteau recited his poem just before he was hanged, and declared that he was proud of what he had done. He had already survived several attempts on his life since his sentencing, but this was his end. Within a decade, many psychiatric professionals had concluded that he should not have been held accountable and that his execution was a mockery of justice. As for Arthur, he had allowed a last-minute appeal to spare Guiteau's life on the grounds of insanity but had refused to overturn the sentence. Hearing that the president would not come to his rescue, Guiteau declared, "Arthur has sealed his doom and the doom of this nation. He and his cabinet are possessed of the devil."

The president and his devil-possessed administration did not pay much attention to Guiteau in these months. The Chinese Exclusion Act was followed by another confrontation over a rivers and harbors bill. The proposed legislation allotted $19 million to purported improvements of the Mississippi levees and Atlantic and Pacific coast harbors, and for easing navigation in several larger lakes. But the largest share of money was for the Mississippi. Nineteen million dollars was a considerable portion of federal outlay in 1882, and nearly 4 percent of government receipts; an equivalent percentage of the federal budget in the early twenty-first century would amount to more than $40 billion. Making sure that the Mississippi levees were maintained was certainly important, and while the states were expected to bear a considerable portion of the expense, so was the federal government. The debates over what role Washington should play in advancing domestic commerce had been heated in the 1820s and 1830s, but after the Civil War the principle wasn't at issue anymore. The size of the appropriation, however, struck most people outside of Congress as absurd.

The 1882 Rivers and Harbors Bill was a prime piece of legislative pork. Just as federal highway money in the twentieth century paid for local contractors and who knows what else, nineteenth-century congressmen viewed river and harbor bills as delicious sources of patronage and influence. The legislation proposed in 1882 would have been a windfall. Each member of Congress was allocated a generous sum to dispense to local businessmen, who in turn would support them in the midterm elections. Those congressmen who favored the reform efforts then making their tortuous way through Capitol Hill opposed the bill, calling it "scandalous and outrageous." Critics outside of Washington took the legislation as proof that the brief interregnum of good government ushered in by Arthur was now over. But to the dismay of many congressional Republicans and not a few Democrats, Arthur, calling the bill an illegitimate use of federal funds, vetoed it in early August.

Congress was winding down for the summer, and few had expected Arthur to reject the bill. The announcement was a dramatic event, and it caused something of a scene in the House of Representatives as various groups huddled in the well of the chamber to deride the president and express amazement at his audacity. In their hearts, many members of Congress had assumed that Arthur would simply be a place keeper, and they were annoyed to find that he actually intended to exercise his constitutional authority.

In his veto message, Arthur acknowledged that "many of the appropriations [were] clearly for the general welfare." Draining the marshlands around the Potomac and improving navigation along the Mississippi were imperative for the health of the nation's commerce. But Arthur charged that too many of the provisions were not for the general welfare and would not promote commerce between the states. Rather, they would benefit only "the particular localities in which it is proposed to make the improvements," and that, declared Arthur, was beyond the rightful scope of the federal government. Why should citizens of several different states be asked to pay for a project that would help only one county of one state, especially at a cost that was substantially greater than any previous bill for river and harbor improvements? Arthur called on Congress to reduce the amount and narrow the range of projects to be funded. While his veto message was hardly stirring rhetoric, it conveyed a sympathy for the reformers that no one, including the reformers themselves, had detected in Arthur before he became president.

Congress responded by promptly overturning the veto, even though some Republicans who initially supported the bill were beginning to suspect that it might prove to be a liability in the fall elections. Most Republicans were in blissful ignorance about the rising tide of reform, but a few discerned which way the wind was blowing. Many southern Democrats supported the bill for the obvious reason that the Mississippi was vital to their economic survival. While Arthur could afford to alienate the Democrats, he was now in danger of losing the support of his own party, much as John Tyler, another vice president vaulted to the presidency, had lost the support of his in 1841. Arthur had gone against his party twice in the space of a few months, having vetoed the exclusion act and now the harbors bill, and by distancing himself from the Stalwart faction and then quietly rewarding Stalwarts once Conkling and Blaine had departed, Arthur had started to make himself a man without a party. That too did not augur well for Republican fortunes in the fall.

Outside of politics, the summer was eventful in other respects. Railroad construction reached an apex, and with that came labor unrest. Steelworkers went on strike, as did railroad freight handlers. P. T. Barnum astonished and delighted New York and the Northeast with Jumbo the Elephant, who was brought across the seas to serve as an exotic wonder in the circus. Thomas Edison and his company were hard at work on a power station that would by summer's end provide New York City with its first supply of electricity and electric lights. And in early September, as the season was winding down, a parade estimated at twenty thousand to thirty thousand people marched through Manhattan to honor the workingman, beginning a tradition soon known as Labor Day.

Almost anyone who could afford to leave Washington in August did so. President Arthur vacationed briefly in Rhode Island and caused a miniscandal when he refused to attend a clambake in Newport. A short while earlier, he had feasted on clams at the Squantum Club near Providence, so it wasn't an issue with the mollusks per se. Nor was it a question of dislike for Newport society. The "City by the Sea" had recently become a playground for the rich, and mansions were springing up on the Cliff Walk. While the Breakers, the seventy-room Vanderbilt mansion, was not yet complete, others were. There was Beechwood, the summer home of the Astors, and there was also the Newport Casino, the exclusive men's club opened in 1880 by James Gordon Bennett, the owner of the *New York Herald*. The casino was the center of the social scene, where drinks and cigars were consumed on cool porches in between leisurely and competitive games of the newest English import, lawn tennis. The first U.S. National Championships (the precursor to the U.S. Open) were held on its courts in 1881. Arthur, however, wasn't interested in physical activity. He had come for some rest and relaxation with his New York set, but his nonappearance at the banquet of the season was nothing if not noticeable. Many wondered why the gentleman president forsook what would surely have been a gastronomic delight surrounded by the leading lights of Newport society.

Though only he and his physician knew it, politics wasn't the only thing ailing the president. Arthur was suffering from Bright's disease, a kidney disorder that had begun to disrupt his entire metabolism. Diagnosed first by the famed British physician Richard Bright, the syndrome caused headaches, puffiness, chronic fevers, and fatigue. The term *Bright's disease* has become anachronistic and actually refers to a wide range of problems. Arthur's glomerulonephritis (as it would now be called) made it difficult for his nephrons to rid his body of toxins. His blood and body were slowly being poisoned by his own digestion. Though the causes of the illness were unclear, in essence, Arthur the gourmand was dying because of his appetites.

In an age before antibiotics or dialysis, the only known treatment was fluid intake and bed rest. Though Bright's disease could be mild or severe, Arthur was afflicted with a severe form. The once ebullient bon vivant found himself tired and cranky. His desire for food was erratic, and while the press was left to speculate bemusedly why the president avoided a clambake, Arthur suffered quietly in his rooms, knowing that there was no cure and that things could only get worse. His own health was precarious, and he feared, rightly, that the health of his party, which he had loved as much as any family, was not much better.

7

Reform

The end of summer brought a return to politics. Reluctantly, Chester Arthur came back to Washington in early September, though he managed to slip out again at the end of the month for a fishing trip to upstate New York. In Utica, he was greeted with the warmth of a hometown boy done good, and he relaxed into the easy embrace of the crowds there. Addressing the well-wishers who turned out to meet his train, he thanked them for giving him a respite from his labors in the nation's capital.

That struck some as odd, coming as it did from a man not known for his labors. As president, Arthur had a reputation for working short hours, and while it is tempting to fob that off to the fatigue brought on by Bright's disease, even before its onset he had never been one for late nights in the office. His critics called him "indolent," and even his supporters noted his disinclination to appear in his office before ten A.M. or to remain later than five. Said one White House clerk years later, Arthur "never did today what he could put off until tomorrow." During his years as president, however, he took no special pleasure in either his leisure or his work. He resented the pressure of reporters to give interviews; he felt imposed upon by callers looking for favors; and he disliked the proximity of his office to his home. As he told one interviewer at the end of his term, "You have no idea how depressing and fatiguing it is to live in the same house where you work. The down-town business man in New York would feel quite differently at the close of his day were he to sit down in the atmosphere of his office to find rest and recreation instead of going uptown to cut loose absolutely from everything connected with his work of the day."

The acrimonious climate in Washington certainly exacerbated the situation. Arthur's honeymoon had all but worn off, and although he personally was not the subject of intense animosities, the fall elections promised another round of factional jousting. Except for the unfortunate Johnson administration, the Republicans had controlled the White House since 1860. They had also dominated Congress for most of that time, save for a brief scare in 1875, and while the past elections had been closely contested by a resurgent Democratic Party, Republicans had come to expect victory. That was a recipe for sloth and corruption, and the Democrats recognized that they had an opportunity to wrest control of Congress.

The Democratic Party was no more cohesive than the Republican. Democrats were divided between Bourbons, who were interested primarily in victory and in a social status quo of limited government and extensive patronage, and reformers, who looked on the entire political system as in need of change. The party was also split between southern and northern wings. Southerners wanted to reestablish an antebellum racial hierarchy that re-created slavery in all but name, and northerners wanted to take advantage of their industrial wealth to extend their reach across the West. In New York, the Democrats were led by the colorless but popular mayor of Buffalo, Grover Cleveland, a Bourbon who stood neither for reform nor against it. How New York went in the midterm elections would be a key litmus test for which party was in the ascendency.

Arthur had spoken in favor of reform in his first address to Congress, but he had shown little inclination to turn honeyed words into legislation. There was a bill stuck in committee that had been sponsored by the Democratic senator George Pendleton of Ohio. The Pendleton Bill directly addressed the issue of civil service reform, and the fact that it came from Pendleton was remarkable. Pendleton had been a pro-slavery Democrat and George McClellan's running mate against Abraham Lincoln in the 1864 presidential election. His career in the Senate was marked by gentility and close ties to the railroads. That hardly set him apart from his fellow senators, most of whom owed a portion of their wealth and success to some railroad, bank, or robber baron. Yet at the end of 1880, he proposed a sweeping revision of civil service rules using British-style exams to create a screening system based entirely on merit. Throughout 1881 and into 1882, the Pendleton Bill was stalled in the limbo of Senate committees. It had the support of the New York Civil Service Reform League and other associations throughout the country, but they had no power to move the bill, and it languished.

While Republicans in Congress went about their business, there were ample signs of public discontent with that business. Arthur had scored points early in his term by supporting the prosecution of one of the major scandals of the post–Civil War era: the Star Route frauds. At the center of the scandal was none other than Stephen Dorsey, the carpetbagger senator who had worked closely with Arthur and the Stalwarts to ensure victory in Indiana during the 1880 election and who had been the object of such fulsome praise by Arthur and Grant at Delmonico's that night in February 1881. Dorsey was implicated in a complicated, lucrative scheme that had defrauded the federal government to the tune of millions of dollars.

Throughout the 1870s, as more of the Native American tribes were defeated by the U.S. Army and as more settlers ventured into the vast space between the Plains and the Sierra Nevada of California, the U.S. Post Office was the only thing that could be counted on to connect them to the states of the East. Occasionally by train, but usually by stagecoach or individual teams of horses, the mail was delivered along more than nine thousand routes that dotted the mostly barren landscapes of what is now Colorado, Arizona, New Mexico, Montana, and the rest.

Some of these routes were serviced by direct employees of the Post Office, which was then by far the largest single source of federal jobs, with over fifty-five thousand workers in 1881. But many of the routes were contracted out to local entrepreneurs, who used the subsidy to settle remote regions. The Wild West of Hollywood never quite existed, but it almost did in the late 1870s and early 1880s, when the saloon, the sheriff, and the post office were the foundations of Main Street. Ranchers ruled domains as large as counties, and they demanded regular mail routes to allow them to do business with the more settled areas of the country. These new communities hovered in a twilight between lawful and lawless, and that meant opportunities for those willing to exploit them. With the power to grant contracts, officials on the postmaster general's staff saw a golden opportunity to skim, and they found a willing and able ally in Dorsey.

The Star Routes got their name from the star or asterisk stamped on the contracts, which was supposed to represent

"certainty, celerity, and security." For Dorsey and his com-
padres, the star could well have stood for graft, profit, and
embezzlement. They found a variety of ways to rob the government. The most lucrative was to award contracts to friends
and family (which was ethically questionable but not, by the
standards of the day, illegal) at a cost that had been approved
by Congress and then have the cost revised sharply upward on
the grounds that the route needed to be upgraded in order to
maintain consistent service. In this fashion, routes that were
originally contracted for thousands became contracts for tens
and even hundreds of thousands of dollars. The fraud was too
blatant to go undetected, and Dorsey and several others were
caught.

Most people assumed that they would evade punishment,
just as the perpetrators of the Crédit Mobilier scheme during
the Grant administration did. Many critics simply shrugged in
weary recognition that people would do such things as long as
they had a decent prospect of getting away with them. Few
expected Arthur to pursue the conviction of Dorsey, and
some suspected that he himself had turned a blind eye or perhaps even profited personally. In part to allay such suspicion,
Arthur instructed the attorney general to prosecute, and in
July 1882 Dorsey and eight other men went on trial. Dorsey
was defended by one of the great lawyers and orators of the
day, the Republican politician Robert Ingersoll, whose stirring
nominating speech for James Blaine at the 1876 Republican
convention had immortalized the senator from Maine as the
"Plumed Knight." The Star Route trial went on and on as hundreds of witnesses were called by the defense in an attempt
to overwhelm the jury with facts. In part because of Ingersoll,
but more because the affair involved some of the most important figures in the national Republican Party, the scandal was

covered with relish by reporters, and day after day the public was treated to detailed accounts of the courtroom drama. In September 1882, the jury acquitted most of the defendants, including Dorsey, and the foreman then alleged that he had been offered bribes. The judge declared a mistrial, and the whole process began again.

While the allegations of jury tampering caused a minor uproar, there was such cynicism about politics that few were surprised. More startling would have been a speedy trial followed by a swift sentence of guilt. But however expected the outcome had been, it added to the widespread discontent with the way things were. Most Republicans then in power failed to notice the shift in public sentiment, and they headed into their state nominating conventions confident about their prospects in the upcoming fall elections.

It wasn't as though there were no signs. True, it was easy enough to dismiss the carping of Henry Adams, or of Godkin and the *Nation* crowd, as elitist braying. And it didn't take undue effort to put the Civil Service Reform League in the same category as the temperance movement or other agglomerations of do-gooders that sought to influence the public policy of the nation from time to time. But other signs should have been heeded. The reformers of the 1870s hadn't disappeared. The Republicans of New York State certainly should have remembered how well Samuel Tilden had done campaigning against the spoils system and finally standing up to the Tweed ring. Republicans throughout the country should have remembered the popular backlash after the economic disaster of the Panic of 1873. And if they had been paying attention, they might have noted the success of Henry George's *Progress and Poverty*, published in 1879.

George had scant reason to suspect that his tract would sell more copies than any book had since Harriet Beecher Stowe's fictional manifesto against slavery in the 1850s. He knew only that every day he was reminded of the yawning gap between the most wealthy and privileged Americans and the rest, and he was certain that such inequality wasn't what the founders had in mind. He wrote *Progress and Poverty* as an expression of his own reservations about the current state of affairs. Poverty was increasing at an even faster rate than prosperity as the rewards of the new industrialism were distributed to very few and the costs borne by very many. George warned that society stood on a precipice. "There is," he wrote, "a vague but general feeling of disappointment; an increased bitterness among the working classes; a widespread feeling of unrest and brooding revolution." The book, initially self-published, quickly sold hundreds of thousands of copies.

The ruling Republicans, along with many Bourbon Democrats, were unpersuaded by the arguments in favor of reforming the political system. They had lived through the economic upheavals of the 1870s and had resisted the more radical calls for change. Eventually, the country had worked its way out of depression, without drastic action from Washington. Labor unrest had crested and then receded. The Republicans of the early 1880s seem to have believed that calls for reform could and should be ignored, and that eventually the critics would run out of steam. Even the mildly liberal *Harper's Weekly* could comment on the eve of the 1882 election that "the last four years of Republican rule have been years of unexampled prosperity. Never have the advantages of a free government been so signally conspicuous. The tide of improvement began with the return . . . to good government, with the complete control of the Republican party in Congress, and the partial restoration of order in the southern States. It grew in the later years of President Hayes' administration and it promises to advance even more under Arthur. Confidence and hope fill the nation." And for those who were being left behind, well, it was a world where the most capable thrived, a world that, at least according to the Yale professor William Graham Sumner, followed the dictates of Charles Darwin's theory of survival of the fittest. Government could do little to change human nature, and attempts at reform, however noble-minded, were doomed to failure.

And so when the polls closed in November and the returns came in, the Republicans were appalled to discover how much they had misread the public mood. Already, they had sustained several setbacks in state legislative elections, most notably in Ohio, but no one had expected a defeat as stunning as the one they suffered on Election Day. They didn't just lose control of the House; they were crushed. They were crushed in states where they had been strong for years, states like Massachusetts, New York, Pennsylvania, New Jersey, and Connecticut. The losses were particularly acute in races for the statehouse. In New York, Democratic Grover Cleveland won the governorship by a huge majority over Arthur's Treasury secretary, Charles Folger. Even the deep pockets of Jay Gould could not buy the New York Republicans into power, though divisions within the state party hadn't helped matters. In Pennsylvania, the ticket sponsored by Senator James Donald Cameron, who had replaced Conkling as the Stalwart spoilsman par excellence, lost by a hundred thousand votes, and Cameron himself lost the backing of the legislature.

In the House of Representatives, nearly forty incumbents were defeated, almost all of them Republicans. That was almost unprecedented. The balance shifted decisively in favor of the Democrats, who in the Forty-eighth Congress would enjoy a majority of nearly two to one in the House. The Democrats gained seventy seats, which was the second largest increase in American history to that point. The only saving grace for the Republicans was that control of the Senate did not change dramatically, and the party held on to its advantage of thirty-eight to thirty-six, with two Readjusters from Virginia. But the damage to the Republicans was hard to overstate. It was, said Thomas Platt, the worst thing to happen to the Grand Old Party in the thirty years since it was created.

Chester Arthur did not escape blame for the party's poor showing. Said the usually warm *New York Times*, "Men seem instinctively to have reached the conclusion that the scheming tricksters who dabble in political affairs for the money there is in them were responsible for the humiliating position in which a great party had been placed." According to one New York Republican grandee, "The reason for the defeat . . . in this state is very apparent. A lot of pot-house politicians headed by President Arthur tried to dictate to the people what they should do. Disgusted with the President and his chosen associates, disgusted with their methods . . . the people have said, 'We have had enough of machines and bosses, and will administer such a rebuke as you deserve, such as you will feel and such as will bring you to your sense.'" The *Chicago Tribune* editorialized, "Pres. Arthur was the worst beaten man in the recent elections." The editors of the *Nation* could scarcely conceal their I-told-you-so glee. The defeat was a symptom of the "evils pervading the party," and unless the president and party leaders did something dramatic to stem the damage, Republicans could be headed for extinction. The only course of action was to heed the message of the electorate: decrease tariffs,

ZACHARY KARABELL

abjure pork projects, and above all pass a bill to abolish the
spoils system and replace it with a professional civil service
chosen on the basis of merit and secure in their jobs regardless
of which party was in power.

More than a few were ungracious in defeat, and there was
the requisite blaming of the press for firing up popular passions. In New York especially, where the Republican candidate
for governor had lost by the greatest margin any candidate ever
had in any state election in U.S. history, Grover Cleveland's
appeal alone was not enough to account for the defeat. The
press made a handy target, but once the accusation had been
made, so what? Holding E. L. Godkin or the *New York Tribune*
responsible did not answer the question of how to win back
alienated voters. Many prominent Republicans still didn't get it
and continued to dismiss calls for reform. The election wasn't
lost because of a popular groundswell, they said. It was lost
for the same reason all elections are lost, because one party outmaneuvered another, because one set of politicians proved
more skillful at manipulating opinion, or because one party
was graced with more dynamic candidates or fewer internal
divisions.

Though some of the party faithful clung to these illusions,
most political leaders concluded that popular backlash against
the spoils system caused the debacle. Within days after the
election, Republicans everywhere had concluded that the
defeat was due primarily to a widespread disaffection with
"bossism." Why this tidal wave had caught the party completely off-guard was an especially sensitive issue. One of
Arthur's close friends, George Bliss, told the *New York Times*
that the election had exposed the Republican Party as a straw
man that had succeeded in the past contests only because its

102

Democratic adversaries were even more disorganized and stupid. Until the fall of 1882, Bliss said, Republicans "could always rely on [their] opponents to make a fatal mistake." But this time, it was the Republicans who had tripped. For months, in papers and in pulpits, out on the hustings and throughout the country, there had been a steady stream of invective directed against bossism and the corruption of the current political system. Yet Republicans had ignored the portents.

Left in shambles, the party snapped to attention. Motivated more by fear than by principle, the Republicans realized that it was vital to stem the damage and prevent the Democrats from consolidating their gains in the future. Within weeks of the defeat, they became zealous converts to the cause of civil service reform. Warner Miller, who had filled Thomas Platt's Senate seat in New York, announced that he favored a civil service bill—"in obedience to the wishes of many of my constituents, expressed to me in letters which I have received from several prominent citizens." Senator John Logan, who was to Illinois what Conkling had been to New York, reversed a decade of opposition to reform and declared his unequivocal support for immediate and radical legislative action to address the issue.

The Democrats, basking in their victory, were ambivalent. What was the point of gaining control if you couldn't enjoy the fruits? Bourbon Democrats hadn't exactly campaigned on a clean government platform, though they had played on popular images of corrupt Republican bosses. Many Democrats were vehemently antagonistic to any changes in the status quo and derided the sudden and hypocritical Republican enthusiasm for "snivel service reform." Democrats had suffered from the spoils system long enough, and now they planned to enjoy the rewards. But though the Democrats had won, the new Congress's term wouldn't begin until the early spring of 1883, and a lame-duck session of the old Congress would meet first. If Republicans were going to seize the mantle of reform, they would have to do it during the lame-duck session or else be saddled with the onus of bossism during the presidential election of 1884.

The result was that Pendleton's civil service reform bill, which had been stuck in committee, was suddenly revived, dusted off, and placed on the fast track to passage. The fact that the bill had been drafted under the auspices of a Democratic senator was awkward for the Republicans. But there wasn't time to draft a new one, and the Pendleton Bill as written covered the main issues. The proposed legislation would create a civil service commission and a board to set standards for an exam and make sure that it was fairly administered. There was heated debate over the nature of these exams. Some legislators feared that if examinations were too difficult, the result would be "an official caste" of mandarins so separate that they would not reflect democratic values. Others worried that if the bar was too low, the whole system could become a sham. The compromise was to make the exams "practical in their character" in order to test "the fitness of candidates."

Exams were imperative for the creation of a professional, merit-based bureaucracy, but unless something could be done to end the old system of patronage, exams wouldn't matter. Recognizing that, the Pendleton legislation outlawed the system of assessments that politicians such as Chester Arthur and Stephen Dorsey had spent careers perfecting. Arthur himself understood that assessments lay at the heart of the spoils system and created an unhealthy link between appointments and fund-raising. As he candidly admitted in a speech during the summer of 1882, it went "without saying that such contributions are not voluntary." The price of gaining an appointment was paying the assessment, and in the harsh light of the November elections, the whole loop was now seen as corrupt.

The Pendleton Bill went up for debate in December 1882. The mood in Congress, gloated Henry Adams, was bleak, and its members had the demeanor of a "pack of whipped boys." Legislators competed to stand in the well of the House and Senate so that they could denounce the spoils system, nod to the wisdom of the electorate and the sagacity of the founders, and declare that henceforth the system would be free of the vices that had come to afflict the body politic. Said Senator Preston Plumb of Kansas, "We are not legislating on this subject in response to our judgement of what is proper to be done, but in response to some . . . judgement which has been expressed outside." And outside, he continued, people were hostile to assessments and would penalize any party that defended them.

The pace of the deliberations was accelerated by the short time frame. Republicans needed to pass a bill quickly, and the Democrats were too ambivalent to halt the momentum either in the House or in the Senate. The main debate occurred in the Senate, and the issue dominated the truncated session. It soon became clear that the two parties had traded places. A number of prominent southern Democrats lined up against the bill, and the Republicans tripped over themselves to support it. In the end, however, most Democrats acquiesced, some because they had been pro-reform for years, others because they were reluctant to stand in the way and face wrathful voters the following year. Just after Christmas, the Senate voted 38 to 5 for the bill, with 33 abstentions. The vote was 155 to 47 in the House, with 87 abstentions. No Republican senators voted against the legislation, and President Arthur signed the bill into law in mid-January 1883.

For more than a decade, reformers had tried to dismantle the spoils system. Though there had been a few victories along the way, the advances had been mostly rhetorical. Like campaign funding a century later, civil service reform was something that every politician had given lip service to and that few politicians wanted to enact. It took the assassination of a president to jump-start the process. Guiteau was not, in truth, a bona fide office seeker, but he thought he was. However deluded he may have been, that belief had driven him to kill Garfield. Arthur then made the issue the centerpiece of his first address to Congress, but the inertia of vested interest and Arthur's own ambivalence halted progress throughout 1882. The Pendleton Civil Service Act mandated reforms that Arthur had resisted when the same reforms were recommended by the Jay Commission, which had investigated Arthur's conduct as head of the customhouse years before. Only the severity of the Republican defeat in the fall of 1882 created the necessary critical mass.

In subsequent years, historians have tried to account for the alacrity of the Republican response. Why did the lame-duck session support the bill? Yes, there was the election of 1884 to consider, but some saw the legislation as a power play by defeated legislators to maintain their patronage networks. Until the new Congress was sworn in, and until the Pendleton Bill became law, the outgoing Republicans could cram the bureaucracy with loyalists who would then be the shock troops for 1884. In the meantime, the Pendleton Act would prevent Democrats from removing the grandfathered Republican appointees. One senator wryly suggested an amendment to describe the act as "a bill to perpetuate in office the Republicans who now hold the patronage of the Government." That may explain why many Democrats did not avidly support the bill, but such an explanation may also be a bit too clever and a bit too cynical. Politics in the 1880s were crass and venal, to be sure, but politicians then as now can be genuinely chastened, and threatened, by sudden electoral defeat. Few things unsettle politicians more than unanticipated reversals at the polls, and, in 1882, Republicans, as well as some Democrats, were alarmed that the public had been so unruly and unpredictable. It seemed prudent to listen to what the people wanted and to give it to them.

The Pendleton Civil Service Act is the most memorable piece of legislation to emerge from Chester Arthur's presidency. Symbolically, it marked a before-and-after moment in American politics. Before, the political system had been controlled by a professional political class that treated elections as contests over patronage. While the great debates over slavery in the 1850s and over Reconstruction in the 1860s determined electoral outcomes at least as much as local bosses, by the 1870s politics had become a closed circle that was largely self-funded. Wealthy industrialists certainly contributed to their party of choice, but elections were primarily paid for by assessments. A small group of party bosses in each municipality and state determined who would get thousands of jobs, which in turn guaranteed income for electoral coffers the next time around. Until the mid- to late 1870s, that was the accepted system, and though reformers decried the abuses, it was just the way things were done.

After the passage of the Pendleton Act, it no longer was. The bill articulated a new standard. Civil servants were to be appointed because of their capacity to do the job, not because of whom they knew and what they could pay. Their performance was to be assessed by objective standards, discerned by examinations. These exams were to be administered by a neutral civil service commission and graded by boards that were unaffiliated with factions. Once appointed, civil servants were to serve society rather than parties. They would no longer be subject to mandatory contributions during elections, and they were given job security so that they could perform their jobs and serve society's needs without having to worry about losing favor with the party bosses.

Its noble intentions notwithstanding, the Pendleton Act was more symbol than substance. Various riders restricted its enforcement to big cities. That meant that rural civil servants, especially those employed by the Post Office, were not affected. In fact, in the immediate aftermath of the law's passage, not much changed. Only between 10 and 20 percent of federal workers fell under the new guidelines, and state patronage networks were left untouched. There were ways to get around the ban on assessments, and outright flouting of the law was not unheard of in the years immediately following. Reformers took the cynical view that once again, politicians had managed to snooker a gullible, idealistic public. Republicans had jumped on the reform bandwagon because they needed political cover, and Democrats had not stood in the way because they couldn't pay the political costs. Both parties, however, connived to limit the damage.

Yet something had shifted. Within twenty years, a professional civil service did develop, and the nature of government in the United States changed dramatically. The Pendleton Act allowed for the birth of the modern bureaucratic state, something that most people take as a mixed blessing, but which has been central to shaping life in this country since the late nineteenth century. Until the latter part of that century, the tasks government was expected to perform could be done by any reasonably competent official. With the increasing complexity of society in the industrial age, tasks multiplied, and specialized needs did as well. Already in 1883, government bureaucracies were being called upon to perform a range of tasks that had been unknown a generation earlier: tariff schedules were becoming more intricate; new industries were growing too fast for either the invisible hand of capitalism or the heavy hand of government to modulate; there were new avenues of territorial expansion that the government wanted to oversee; millions of Civil War veterans were expecting pensions; economic might at home was leading to foreign policy forays abroad; and higher levels of education and life expectancy resulted in more people demanding a more equitable and transparent government.

Civil service reform was an early expression of the impulses that would coalesce in the early twentieth century to create the Progressive movement. The Pendleton Act was a vital step toward a new view of government. No longer would it be seen primarily as an adjunct of business or the tool of elites. Instead, government became known as the protector of the common good. Civil service reform was, as historian Richard Hofstadter has written, one of those moments that crop up periodically in American history when people launch "moral crusades" to "restore absolute popular democracy . . . destroy the political machines and put an end to corruption." A professional civil service was a necessary prerequisite to democracy and good government. Who would be the ultimate master of those Post Office officials and Interior Department appointees: a

boss who owed his position to the robber barons and corpora-
tions and patronage, or the people of the United States, for
whom the country was supposedly created and for whose
rights the recent Civil War had supposedly been fought? Of
course, it was not that simple. It never is. But the current of
high dudgeon against any system that smacks of privilege,
favoritism, and ill-gotten gains has always flowed through
American society, and it still does, dammed up and blocked on
occasion, and overflowing the banks of reason and balance on
others.

For those who bemoan the growth of government in our
day, the Pendleton Act might be seen as a step down the road
to perdition. After all, it facilitated the vast expansion of the
federal bureaucracy. Even those who don't like government,
however, can probably appreciate that insofar as some government is a necessary evil, it's better for society that it be administered in a professional manner. Competence is desirable as
well, but corruption is not a recipe for a stable society.

Presidential leadership was not central to the passage of the
Pendleton Act, and though Arthur's signature was necessary,
that was the extent of his active role. The bill was the culmina-
tion of more than a decade of pressure by reformers. Its cham-
pions astutely used the assassination of Garfield as proof that
the spoils system could be lethal to the stability of the republic. The Republican electoral debacle of 1882 further undermined the opponents of reform and created a sense of urgency.
Even so, Arthur could have done much to muddy the waters.
He could have threatened to veto the bill, and used that threat
to delay passage. He was, after all, the spoilsman who became
president, and no one expected him to be an advocate for civil
service reform. Once again, however, Arthur had an astute
sense of public mood, and just as he had used his veto to

thwart the worst of Congress, he now used his signature pen to endorse the best it could offer. Its best in 1883 left much to be desired, but the Pendleton Act, for all its flaws, forever altered the complexion of the U.S. government. It put the old spoils system on a path to obsolescence and it was a necessary prelude to the government-led reforms of the Progressive era and beyond.

8

Travels, Tariffs, and Travails

After the passage of the Pendleton Act, Arthur would be president for two more years. Of course, he didn't know that at the time, and he held out some faint hope of securing his party's nomination in 1884 and then winning the election in his own right. But as early as the beginning of 1883, it was apparent to him and to most others that his chances were slim. James Blaine had increased his stature since his departure from the cabinet, and though Arthur was proving to be a surprisingly competent president, he did not control the national party.

There was nothing unusual about Arthur's questionable standing as 1884 approached. In 1880, Hayes had not won renomination. For his final two years, Arthur was very much a lame duck. No national crisis demanded action. The economy began to soften, but the government was running an immense surplus of over $100 million a year. While partisan divisions made it hard to agree on how to spend it, there was little public pressure to figure it out. The reformers had been temporarily sated by the Pendleton Civil Service Act, and though labor unrest was rising, it hadn't reached the crisis proportions that it would later in the decade. Consciously or not, Arthur took advantage of the relative calm and spent large portions of 1883 traveling the country. He also paid more attention to foreign policy and to the strength of the U.S. military. By early 1884, no one expected him to be a force at the Republican convention, and he spent the last fifteen months of his administration watching as Blaine divided the party even more.

In January 1883, Arthur could not have known that this was his future, but he would not have been surprised. He hadn't sought the presidency, and he didn't derive pleasure from it. He had been wealthy in the 1870s and enjoyed the perks when he was married and secure in his life in New York City. Living in the White House was not the fishbowl experience it would later become, but Arthur never felt at home in the executive mansion. He had no particular passion for being president, and that made the job not only tiring (which it would have been anyway) but also boring. He had no pressing vision for the country that consumed his ambition, and the party that he had dedicated the past thirty years to was turning away from him. He had not inherited Conkling's mantle and could not even claim to lead the Stalwarts. And physically, Bright's disease and years of lavish food and a sedentary lifestyle were taking their toll. Arthur was chronically exhausted. Had modern psychology existed, he would probably have been diagnosed as depressed. At the very least, he was not loving his life.

And so he followed Horace Greeley's injunction and went west, eventually. In the first months of 1883, he supported the formation of a tariff commission. Tariff policy was one of the most heated issues confronting the country. By the 1880s, advocates of high tariffs reviled advocates of low tariffs almost as much as abolitionists had detested slave owners. The argument for high duties on imported manufactured goods was simple: unless they were protected, American businesses could not compete with European manufacturers. The result earlier in the century had been stiff import duties on everything from shoes and steel to clothing and furniture. But over the course of several decades, American industry had become competitive and hugely profitable, and that aggravated those who had always wanted lower tariffs: farmers and workers.

Higher tariffs didn't just protect American industries from foreign competition. They also allowed businesses to charge higher prices domestically. As industrialists became wealthier and lived more opulently, consumers became angrier. From the perspective of farmers or of settlers in the West, high tariffs were a way for eastern captains of industry to gouge the consumer. At the same time, people who opposed high tariffs on manufactured goods often supported them on raw materials. The farmers who grew cotton didn't want foreign competition any more than the owners of textile and steel mills did. Southerners demanded heavy taxes on Indian and Egyptian cotton, and Ohioans wanted stiff duties on imported wool, and these demands in turn angered the bankers and owners of factories, who felt they were being unfairly taxed to subsidize rural America. Neither side grasped their mutual dependence and instead saw the contest in zero-sum terms. In between these two bitterly opposed camps was a moderate middle that objected to the current tariff system because it was inefficient. Some industries thrived under protectionism, others did not, and many people were troubled by the complexity and irrationality of the tax system.

In general, Democrats, who were popular among the working class and in the South, opposed high tariffs, and Republicans, and especially Stalwarts, supported them. Given that the Senate was evenly divided, neither side emerged from the tariff debates with a clear victory. Arthur settled into a now-comfortable role of the moderate who suggested courses of action but did not leap into the fray. The result was predictable. In March, Congress passed a bill that altered a number of specific duties but kept the overall average essentially unchanged. The bill was promptly, and cynically, called "the Mongrel Tariff," because no one could, or wanted to, claim responsibility for its unwieldy series of provisions. As one journal wryly observed, "There was ample evidence that the result was satisfactory to no considerable class of citizens." With rates unchanged, the government continued to run a surplus, and Arthur's reputation suffered because of the widespread sense that he had been a passive bystander.

Debates about the size and scope of tariffs became more heated in subsequent years, along with issues about the valuation of the dollar relative to gold and to silver. The passage of the Mongrel Tariff settled nothing. Had they been given a crystal ball, Democrats and populists might have been dismayed to learn that the Mongrel Tariff was the best they would do for the next twenty years. Future tariff battles were won decisively by protectionists in favor of American manufacturing. For obvious reasons, the robber barons were not interested in free trade, except as a theory to debate over dinner. They were in the business of creating American versions of industries that already existed across the Atlantic, and they needed, or at least demanded, a barrier from European competition. Free trade was left to the British, and in the meantime, American industry rose to a dominant position internationally, aided by a government that shielded it at every turn from real or perceived threats from foreign competitors.

The concern that American industry could be fatally undermined by other countries coincided with a sudden anxiety about the state of the military. Though U.S. ventures abroad were limited to commerce, a vocal group of influential men were acutely aware of how much the military strength of the country had eroded since the Civil War. While the army maintained some funding because of the Indian wars, the navy had all but collapsed. In less than twenty years since the end of the Civil War, it had lost almost 90 percent of its ships. It was, according to the *Nation*, "a satirical semblance of a navy." Its five first-class ships were obsolete; its second-class ships were rotting; and more than half the remaining ships were unseaworthy or rusted beyond repair. Not only were there no adequate steel-clad warships, there weren't even sufficient wooden steamers and support vessels to field a credible defense. That was all the navy had been expected to do, yet it was no longer capable of the most minimal task of keeping the country and its merchant marine secure against possible attacks.

Unspoken was the fact that there were no immediate threats to American maritime security. No Latin American nation challenged American supremacy in the hemisphere, and European expansion was focused on Africa and Asia. The United States had thrived economically as its navy deteriorated, so the call for a massive shipbuilding campaign had to appeal to pride and to the nascent desire of a strong nation to become stronger. Arthur's secretary of the navy, the ardent Half-Breed William Chandler of New Hampshire, made it his mission to convince Congress to spend some of the surplus to transform the United States into a country able to project its power abroad.

It was an undertaking that Arthur emphatically supported. He embraced the plan to build ships designed for offense and attack. He had alluded to the idea in his first address to Congress, and he kept mentioning it until he left the White House. As collector, he had come to appreciate that a strong navy was not just a vital tool of foreign policy but also part of a country's image abroad. Chandler and Arthur yearned for a navy that could float proudly in the company of the British, but in reality, their actual proposals were modest. Compared to Theodore Roosevelt, Arthur had a fairly circumscribed vision of the navy as a symbol of power. But without Arthur, Roosevelt and McKinley might not have had a navy capable of annihilating the Spanish in 1898. Supported by Arthur, Chandler submitted a proposal to Congress late in 1882 for three steel-armored cruisers, and the plan quickly won support. The appropriation was signed at almost the same time as the Mongrel Tariff. The amount was in the low millions, and the ships were not finished for several years. The navy continued to attract the derision of foreign commentators as well as of enterprising journalists who were on the lookout for scandalous stories about government incompetence. But the tide, so to speak, had shifted.

These steps to build a modern navy did not attract as much attention as the tariff or civil service reform. Outside of elite circles, few people were even aware that the appropriation had been made. But the attention paid at the time wasn't commensurate with the importance of the decision. Until the last decades of the nineteenth century, the federal government thought of the navy mostly as a defensive weapon. Even in the expansionary heyday of the 1840s, when people loudly proclaimed America's manifest destiny to bestride the continent, acquire Mexico and Cuba, and dominate the Americas, the size of the military had been small. Americans had never been comfortable with the standing armies of Europe, and absent some military threat or specific goal, the tendency had been to let the military dwindle, as it did in the decades after the Civil War.

The decision, however tentative, to enlarge the navy in a time of peace was an inkling of things to come. Elites in the United States could not help but notice that the Europeans were rapidly colonizing the globe. Even Arthur, whose interest in foreign affairs seems to have been limited to his enthusiasm for English novelists, would have met European visitors and absorbed some of their worldview. Not only was the U.S. Navy weak, but even the merchant marine had not kept current, and as America's trade with the world grew, the percentage of that trade carried by U.S. ships shrank. Slowly, it began to dawn on leading Americans that their economic power was not reflected in international prominence. The United States was becoming a first-rank power economically, but it remained a nonplayer in world affairs.

Building a navy was a step. It would take several more years before American leaders started to use that power more aggressively. Fortunately, or not, depending on one's view of American imperialism, when the clamor to extend American influence abroad grew louder in the 1890s, there was a navy capable of doing it. In the interim, under Arthur, Secretary of State Frelinghuysen started to insert the United States into the politics of Central and South America.

Blaine had begun that process in 1881 by calling for a Pan-American conference. Modeling the meeting after the various diplomatic congresses that Europeans had organized in past centuries, Blaine looked on the Pan-American congress as a way to establish the United States as the moderator of trade and diplomacy throughout the Western Hemisphere. He also recognized that unless the United States stepped in to claim leadership, European powers would claim it instead. British trade with South America was accelerating, and many Latin American countries had valuable natural resources, from guano to copper to cattle, that hungry industrialists craved. Blaine's resignation from the cabinet put plans for the conference on hold, and the meeting didn't convene until 1889. Frelinghuysen, however, continued Blaine's policies.

That entailed diplomatic involvement in distant conflicts. The Pacific War had raged between Peru and Chile since 1879, and Frelinghuysen, with Arthur's full support, stepped in to mediate. He also devoted considerable energy to bilateral tariff negotiations. Trade had to increase for American influence to increase, and Frelinghuysen worked quietly on reciprocity agreements with individual countries and governments whereby the United States would lower its tariffs on specified imported goods in return for lower tariffs on its exports. In this way, Frelinghuysen, and thus the Arthur administration, was able to circumvent some of the restrictions of the Mongrel Tariff. And, of course, there were numerous business relationships that the administration facilitated. The State Department played the role of the modern-day Commerce Department, and consuls did what they could to smooth the path for American entrepreneurs doing business abroad. The most promising deal of the day was a concession to construct a canal linking the Pacific and the Atlantic using the flat land and multiple lakes of Nicaragua. Other routes were also in play. Already, the French entrepreneur Ferdinand de Lesseps, father of the Suez Canal, had obtained a concession and formed a company to build a canal across the Isthmus of Panama. Eventually, Panama won out, controlled by Americans and not the French, but in Arthur's day, talk of a Nicaraguan canal was enough to send investors into frenzied dreams.

The primary arena of American expansion, however, remained the West. The Native Americans of the Plains had resisted the advance until the mid-1870s, but the Bighorn

Mountains of Montana and the Black Hills and Badlands of South Dakota could shelter them only so long. By the time Arthur became president, Montana, Wyoming, Nebraska, and the Dakotas were under the firm control of settlers and the army, and the mines of Bozeman and the plains of Wyoming were filling with ranchers and miners. In the Southwest, the Apache, Comanche, and Navaho tribes, led in part by Geronimo, tried to remain autonomous, but the uneasy coexistence between them and white settlers was short-lived. In his inaugural address, Arthur praised the army for the surrender of Sitting Bull on the Canadian border, and he expressed the hope that future confrontations could be avoided. He ordered the army to negotiate treaties first, and called for the integration and assimilation of Native Americans, in order "to absorb them into the mass of our citizens, sharing their rights and holden to their responsibilities." He supported the establishment of Indian schools to teach American laws and customs, and he urged Congress to pass legislation that would rationalize the haphazard state of relations between the United States and various tribes. Congress, however, did nothing until 1887, when the Dawes Act tried to make homesteaders out of former Indian warriors and their families.

Though his approach was reasoned and sober, Arthur spoke from an Olympian detachment about the actual realities on the ground. Settlers and territorial officials were uninterested in accommodating their ambitions and greed to the needs of the increasingly scattered and weak tribes. His conciliatory Indian policy notwithstanding, Arthur was more compelled by the landscape of the West than by the plight of the Native Americans who lived there. He had last been exposed to the frontier in Kansas in the 1850s, and he was eager to survey the tens of millions of acres that were being rapidly carved up and settled.

He felt the same pull of the West that Americans had experienced at least since the expedition of Lewis and Clark. Arthur had known Albert Bierstadt in New York and had, along with thousands of others, gazed in delight at Bierstadt's immense canvases depicting the grandeur of nature in Yellowstone Park and the Sierra Nevadas of California. Painters such as Bierstadt brought a dramatic slice of the romantic West to the jaded East, and now that he was president, Arthur wanted to go and see for himself. There wasn't much keeping him in Washington.

Before the West, however, he took a trip to Florida in the spring. This was not the Florida of retirement communities and condominiums. It was a flat land of orange groves and swamps. Arthur went by private railcar to Savannah, Georgia, and then on to Jacksonville by train. In theory, the trip was supposed to be good for the ailing president's health, but the hot regions of northern Florida did nothing to lift his spirits or heal his body. He developed a high fever, and for a few hours surgeons feared he might not survive. The attack was clearly related to his kidney disease. To add insult to injury, Arthur was then criticized in various papers for taking a meaningless "junket," and this even before he had left on the far more extensive trip planned for later in the summer. Arthur's friends tried to downplay the illness and claimed that the president had been only slightly "indisposed." Arthur brushed off reporters and denied that he had been sick at all. He was not the last chief executive who tried to conceal the full extent of his health problems from the public.

The following month, Arthur returned to New York City to spend a few days at his home and at the Fifth Avenue Hotel. He was met by wildly enthusiastic crowds—not because he was president, however, but because he had come to celebrate the opening of what was then the greatest technical wonder of

the United States: the Brooklyn Bridge. For a few days in late
May, the city was a continuous party. The bridge was lauded
as a symbol of the emerging power, creativity, and industrious-
ness of the American people, and in an age when rhetoric slid
easily into hyperbole, speeches in honor of the bridge and its
engineers were excessively florid. On May 24, 1883, amid fire-
works, cannons, military parades, confetti, and the cacophony of
brass bands, Arthur and the mayors of New York and Brooklyn
inaugurated the span linking the two large cities. While Arthur
enjoyed the festivities, the crowds did get out of hand, and
several people were trampled when the throngs crossed the
bridge.

In July, the president set out for Yellowstone Park, with a
retinue that included General Philip Sheridan, who had led the
recent campaigns against the Plains Indians, and Secretary of
War Robert Todd Lincoln. Lincoln had proven to be an able
head of the department responsible for the Indian wars, and
though the area to be visited by the presidential party was no
longer a war zone, the annihilation of Custer at Little Bighorn
was only a few years past. Yellowstone had been made the first
national park in 1872, well before the pacification of the Sioux.
This was an act of extraordinary foresight on the part of the
Grant administration, which recognized that soon enough, it
was not the settlers who would be threatened but the wilderness that they were settling. The creation of Yellowstone was
an early act of preservation. Already, Americans of the latter
part of the nineteenth century were feeling the nagging sense
of loss that came with conquering the continent, and Yellowstone was intended as a shrine to an age when the land was
untouched by "civilization" and business.

It wasn't until the defeat of Sitting Bull that the route to the
park was considered safe, and President Hayes had ventured

through Wyoming on the way to California soon after, in the summer of 1880. Arthur's trip came in the midst of a mini-boom of the Yellowstone tourist industry. Lodges were being built, and intrepid travelers took the railroad and then hooked up with the Bozeman trail, which would lead them into the stunning park. One of the prime destinations was the Yellowstone Falls, recently the subject of one of Bierstadt's massive canvases. Another attraction was a plume of water that spouted high into the air at such regular intervals that the *New York Times* described it as "an old faithful geyser."

The first leg of Arthur's excursion was a train ride to Chicago. The presidential party traveled in a specially outfitted Pullman car, and then changed trains for Cheyenne, Wyoming. From there it was a 350-mile loop by horseback to the park and back. At Fort Washakie, near the Wind River, Arthur was treated to an Arapahoe ceremonial dance followed the next day by a mock battle between Shoshones and Arapahoes. While he was not hailed as a conqueror, there wasn't much difference between him and those forgotten Roman emperors of the third century who periodically journeyed to the frontier. Arthur took every opportunity he could to go fishing. He had trawled the lakes of upstate New York, and he was an eager angler in Wyoming and spent hours fishing for river trout. After the Wind River, the party headed for the Snake River and Jackson Lake, where there was more fishing and fresh, crisp air that invigorated the increasingly lethargic president. Throughout these weeks, the party enjoyed perfect weather, and the high point for Arthur was fishing in a Yellowstone tributary and catching thirty-five trout that weighed more than forty pounds in total.

The trip was soon being called, somewhat mockingly, "the Presidential Sporting Excursion of 1883." It had taken months to organize. Camping spots had been scouted well in advance by U.S. troops under Sheridan's command, and the logistics were complicated. The region was still wild, and it would have been embarrassing if the president had been lost in the woods. The area was mostly uninhabited, now that the Indian tribes had been removed and millions of buffalo slain by settlers. That meant that the president's retinue had to carry a month's worth of food and supplies, and that added up to a party of dozens. The official cost of the trip was not published but, with the government surplus, there were no serious objections. Arthur was away from Washington for almost two months, and no one seems to have cared one way or the other. The Yellow-stone adventure made for good copy in national newspapers, but it was indicative of Arthur's marginalization that politics went on as if he had never left, or as if he had never been in the White House in the first place.

The fact that he was president was not forgotten, at least not by several misguided but enterprising cowboys who planned to kidnap him on the outskirts of Yellowstone. Hatched by a Texan desperado, several Italian railroad workers, one Indian guide, and dozens of accomplices, the scheme was to spirit Arthur to caves in the mountains and then conduct ransom negotiations. They hoped to get Arthur's wealthy friends to pay five hundred thousand dollars to obtain the president's safe release. The organizers were never caught, and the whole thing may have been nothing but a rural legend. Yet reports of the plot were widely disseminated. It confirmed the image of the lawless West that had already taken root in popular imagi-nation, and it added luster to Arthur's trip.

The president returned to Washington in mid-September refreshed, relaxed, in good spirits and health, and "looking bet-ter than ever," according to one correspondent. Congress had of course met during the spring and would convene during the fall, to take up bills dealing with governing the territory of Alaska and tweaking the tariff schedule. Before Arthur's trip, the long-drawn-out Star Route trials had finally come to an end with the jury finding all of the defendants, including Dorsey, not guilty. The fact that Arthur had insisted on the government prosecuting the case even after the first mistrial had helped his image, but the fact that the Justice Department had failed to obtain a conviction after more than a year and a half of effort did not. With the Star Route cases finished, Arthur had no high-profile cause and no legislative agenda to push, and his lack of clear goals contributed to his dwindling chances in the upcoming 1884 election.

In November 1883, however, Arthur was given a chance to rise to the occasion by the Supreme Court. In one of the worst travesties ever handed down by that august body, the Court declared the Civil Rights Act of 1875 unconstitutional.

While Arthur's solicitor general had not exactly conducted a stirring defense of the act, the ruling of the Court set back the cause of civil rights for decades. The Court doesn't deserve the entire blame. With the end of Reconstruction in 1877, most blacks in the South were relegated to a twilight status between freedom and servitude. Their standing in the North was better, but everywhere they were second-class citizens whose rights were frequently ignored or violated. The Civil Rights Act of 1875 had banned discrimination and segregation in public facilities like hotels, but in the Civil Rights Cases of 1883, the Supreme Court said that the federal government did not have the power to protect "private rights." Congress could mandate that states not pass laws that violated the Fourteenth Amendment, but other than that there was nothing that government could do to prevent individuals from discriminating against other individuals. Blacks had been freed from slavery, wrote Justice Joseph Bradley, and made into "mere citizens" subject to the same whims and personal injustices as all other citizens.

Along with *Plessy v. Ferguson* in 1896, the Civil Rights Cases of 1883 made it possible to create a segregated, racial caste system in the South. The ruling rested on a strict interpretation of the limits of government power to legislate private behavior, and it was a constitutionally defensible decision. In terms of its effect, however, it left blacks without full rights as citizens; in that respect, it was utterly indefensible.

Many at the time recognized the import of the decision, and few were as eloquent as Chester Arthur. He had become an ardent opponent of slavery in the 1850s, and he believed that the Civil War had been fought for the principles later enshrined in the Fourteenth Amendment. In his estimation, the Court, along with a bitter and angry white South, had now betrayed those principles. "It was the special purpose of the amendment," Arthur said in a message to Congress in the wake of the decision, "to insure to members of the colored race the full enjoyment of civil and political rights." The Civil Rights Act of 1875 had been passed for the express purpose of allowing freed slaves to enjoy those rights unimpeded by state laws. In what was for Arthur an unconscionable ruling, the Supreme Court rendered the act null and void. Though he was not willing to flout the decision, he told Congress that he would support legislation to redress what the Court had done. Congress did no such thing, and it would be nearly seventy-five years before that body did anything to reverse the tide of segregation.

As with so much in Arthur's life, we are left with only opaque glimpses into his inner world. His public message objecting to the Court's stance suggested a man who had been and remained deeply committed to the cause of racial equality. But there are few testimonies or letters or later reminiscences by friends and supporters to provide more nuance and detail. Did Arthur curse what the justices had done? Did he quietly shake his head and confess his sorrow to his sister? Did he sit with his nearly teenage daughter and discuss these issues with her? Did he gather friends at the White House to commiserate? We'll never know. We are left to fill in many other blanks as well. Arthur was doing daily battle with a kidney disorder that was becoming progressively worse. That had to affect his mood and behavior, and the fact that his influence was receding as the election of 1884 approached could not have been easy to accept, even if he did lack a strong affection for the presidency. He may not have reveled in the job, but throughout his life he had taken pride in maintaining his dignity and the respect of his peers. As Washington turned away from him and toward the next presidential election, he was left with a drafty house in a city not his own. Chester Arthur at the end of 1883 had a daughter who depended on him and a son making his own way in the world. He had seen the wonders of the West and the man-made marvel of the Brooklyn Bridge. He had traveled through a country that he nominally governed, and returned to Washington only to be reminded that he was a caretaker and that no matter how well he did, he would soon be shown the door.

9

The Final Days

Though many were prepared to write him off, Chester Arthur had no intention of slinking away. He believed that he had acquitted himself honorably and that he deserved another term. The Republican Party was more fractured than it had been at any time since its founding in the 1850s, yet Arthur could legitimately claim that he had done a more than decent job steering the party in the wake of Garfield's assassination and after the disastrous midterm elections of 1882. Though he had no zeal for the nomination, he wasn't prepared to withdraw as if he were an embarrassment.

While Arthur had his supporters, James Blaine was clearly the front-runner. Blaine had been planning for the convention of 1884 since he resigned as secretary of state in 1881. Others would say that he had been planning for longer than that, and that his failure to secure the nomination in 1876 and 1880 had only made him hungrier for the one prize that had eluded him. His power and sway were undiminished, and without a Conkling or Grant or a strong Stalwart faction standing in his way, he appeared quite formidable.

Even after his resignation from Arthur's cabinet, Blaine had left his stamp on the administration. At the end of 1883, Arthur gave his annual message to Congress and again devoted considerable attention to foreign affairs and tariffs. Listeners couldn't help but recognize that Arthur and then Frelinghuysen had followed the course initially charted by Blaine, especially when it came to reciprocity with the nations of South America. Arthur also drew attention to the continued surplus, even with spending on the navy and various other federal programs. Blaine had begun to circulate a vague plan that called for returning the surplus to the states, and Arthur in his address did not offer any concrete alternatives. Going into 1884, therefore, Blaine had the momentum.

A Blaine presidency was no more acceptable to wide swaths of the Republican Party in 1884 than it had been in 1876 or 1880. Blaine was a charismatic, polarizing figure, and liberal Republicans decided that they'd rather see a bland but honest Democrat in the White House. Arthur was only marginally more acceptable. Though he had gone a considerable way to mollify the reformers, he had never convinced the more zealous liberals that he sincerely embraced reform. In response to Blaine's ascendency, liberal Republicans such as former senator and interior secretary Carl Schurz and George William Curtis (who was once called "the most distinguished American citizen in public life who has never held office") splintered from the party and decided to support the Democratic nominee as long as he was less tainted than Blaine. The splinter group was called, by some clever cynic, "Mugwumps," which was an Algonquin word that technically meant "chieftain" but implied a foolish self-importance. The Mugwumps were precursors to the Progressives of the early 1900s. Their ranks were filled with the same reformers who had crusaded for civil service legislation, and they still believed that government was controlled by factions who acted not for the benefit of the country but for their own selfish enrichment.

Though he was unacceptable both to the liberal reformers who formed the Mugwumps and to the party bosses who turned to Blaine, Arthur did have backers, especially in New York. But he wasn't nearly strong enough in his home state to be seen as a formidable challenge to Blaine. He was treated only semiseriously by Godkin and the *Nation*, and he lost the backing of the once-loyal *New York Times*. He was being held responsible for the decline of the Republican Party in New York, and with his chances of even receiving the support of the New York delegation uncertain, his prospects for gaining the nomination were bleak. The fact that this conclusion was drawn by the *Times*, which had been a sturdy supporter of Arthur since his days in the customhouse, was not auspicious. According to the paper, Arthur had endorsed civil service reform but wasn't trusted by the reformers, and he had done just enough to alienate the defenders of the old system. He may have been "a most skillful politician," and he may have had a loyal following amid the party faithful, but, concluded the *Times*, "there is one fact that these gentlemen ignore. Mr. Arthur cannot be elected."

Godkin's *Nation* agreed but praised the president's administration for being "discreet, conservative and cleanly. It will not suffer by comparison with any of its predecessors since Lincoln. Indeed it is above the average of post-bellum administration in point of respectability." That said, Arthur was still a mortally hobbled candidate. "President Arthur has yielded just enough to the reformers . . . to put the Machine managers and war-horses in low spirits. He has not yielded enough to win the confidence of the other side. . . . The conflict between the old and new systems of government is as irrepressible as the conflict between slavery and freedom was twenty-five years ago. No public man can serve both. He must chose, and abide the consequences of his choice."

Arthur had fallen into a trap that is usually fatal to politicians: he had lost his base. Having spent his entire political career as part of one faction, he had earned the near-permanent distrust of competing factions and of the opposing Democrats. Having then taken a step away from his faction as president, he alienated the only solid support he had, and he had not been nearly active or passionate enough about reform to gain the backing of the liberal Republicans. Even if he had, that group was too marginal in the Republican Party to propel him or any other candidate into the White House. Arthur had governed more effectively than most had imagined possible in 1881, but that wasn't enough to win the nomination.

The Republicans were divided as they headed into their convention in June 1884, as they had been in 1880 and in 1876. For the first time in sixteen years, however, Grant wasn't part of the picture. Alive but ailing and bankrupt, he was no longer a viable candidate, and the party was worse for his absence. Though he had not been an exemplary president, after he left the White House he had been a unifying, respected force in an otherwise fractious party. With Grant no longer in the field, Arthur was one of several contenders, and while his chances were slim, he received praise from some unexpected sources. Said Mark Twain, "I am but one in 55,000,000; still, in the opinion of this one-fifty-five-millionth of the country's population, it would be hard to better President Arthur's administration. But don't decide till you hear from the rest." The rest didn't matter nearly as much as the few, and the nomination, like others before and those for many years after, rested not on popular opinion but on the peculiar dynamics of party power brokers.

Though Arthur did well on the first ballot, his support quickly faded. Some New Yorkers voted for him out of respect, knowing that he didn't have the votes to win and that in subsequent ballots he would become a nonfactor. They were right. Blaine was too strong, no matter how much animosity he generated, and this time, finally, he received the nomination. Arthur graciously promised to do what he could to help Blaine and the party, but from the moment he became the candidate, Blaine proved to be as polarizing as his detractors had feared. Liberal Republicans, the derisively named Mugwumps, followed through on their threat and supported the Democratic nominee, Grover Cleveland of New York. The subsequent campaign was an ugly partisan contest. Godkin, who was not alone in believing that Blaine was far less electable than Arthur, spent much of the year adopting an I-told-you-so snigger.

The campaign of 1884 was one of the uglier contests in U.S. history. Both sides resorted to crude character assassination. Blaine was derailed because of a stash of old letters. The "Mulligan letters," named after the recipient, dated from the time of the Crédit Mobilier scandal in 1872. Blaine's tangential connection to the scandal through investments in an Arkansas railroad had been public record since 1876, when the letters had first been used against him. Now that he was on the verge of the presidency, the letters were dredged up again and used to devastating effect. Blaine had ended several of the missives with the instruction "Burn this letter!" Though they had been written by Blaine to exonerate himself, taken out of context they proved his opponents' worst fears that he was not only corrupt but devious and Machiavellian. In an act of piling-on, Blaine was dubbed the "Continental Liar from the State of Maine!" by gleefully malicious delegates at the Democratic convention in July. In retaliation, Cleveland was then subjected to a merciless attack on his own character. He was a bachelor who had carried on an affair that had resulted in a child, and he admitted as much during the campaign. Although that didn't lose him the support of his party, it did lead to an inventive bit of Republican doggerel accompanied by cartoons that showed an infant wailing from its pram, "Ma! Ma! Where's my Pa?" After the election, the Democrats gleefully added, "Gone to the White House. Ha! Ha! Ha!"

A campaign defined by Mulligan letters and malicious rhyming couplets was the perfect iteration of what the reformers had been saying for years. The Arthur administration was reduced to a bystander, and those responsible for covering Washington politics turned once again to describing White House dinners and Arthur's impeccable gustatory skills. The election itself was deemed only marginally more interesting than the arrangement of the White House dining room. As it turned out, the only thing dramatic about the election, other than Cleveland's thin margin of victory, was that a Democrat won both the electoral and popular vote, and for the first time since before the Civil War, the Republicans were voted out of the White House. Perhaps the only vindication for Arthur was that Cleveland defeated Blaine in New York. A banquet at Delmonico's hosted before the election by Gould, Carnegie, Astor, and the richest men of the city to garner support for Blaine had attracted even more negative publicity than Arthur's Delmonico's banquet more than three years before. Dubbed

"Mammon's Homage," the evening probably didn't lose New York for the Republicans, but it was a perfect metaphor for a decadent party and its candidate.

Arthur had done what he could to help the Republican ticket. He had gone to New York at the height of the campaign to lend his advice and expertise to Blaine's managers. Meeting with them in the same suite of the Fifth Avenue Hotel that had seen so much, he announced, "[I] want this ticket elected. I am a Republican." He reminded Blaine's men that they should be careful about what they promised to whom, and he pointed to the chair where Garfield had sat during the conference with Arthur and guaranteed rewards for Conkling and the Stalwarts. The result had been a chaotic Garfield administration, defined in its first months by internecine warfare among the Republicans. And that, Arthur said, had weakened the party and paved the way for the strength of the Democrats in New York State. The reaction of Blaine and his inner circle wasn't recorded, but given how they ran their campaign, it seems doubtful that they took Arthur's lesson to heart.

After Cleveland's victory, the remainder of Arthur's term was occupied with his final message to Congress and the conclusion of a treaty with Nicaragua for the construction of a canal. There was also talk in New York of nominating Arthur for one of the state's two U.S. Senate seats, but Arthur decided that he preferred to retire to his home on Lexington Avenue and resume his old law practice. The final ball at the White House was conducted with the brio that Washington society had come to expect from Arthur, and Cleveland was warmly welcomed by the outgoing president and his sister.

The Gentleman Boss ended his term with a gentlemanly gesture. Early in his tenure, Arthur had refused to back a bill in

Congress to restore Grant to the rank and salary of an active general, even though Arthur had spent much of his life in service of Grant's career. In the three years since this rebuff, Grant's health had deteriorated along with his finances. As 1885 began, the former general and president was riddled with cancer and besieged with creditors. Whether or not Arthur regretted his earlier decision, he recommended to Congress that a special bill be passed to give Grant a pension worthy of all that he had done for the Union. The last act signed by Arthur created an exception for Grant so that he could receive a considerable salary in his final months. Congressmen stood and applauded when the bill was passed. Arthur the Stalwart had engaged in the ultimate act of rewarding a partisan; he had made sure that a loyal party man was duly rewarded for his service. But in the case of Ulysses Grant, it was a reward that few could begrudge. Grant had done his best for his country and his party. If the boss system was, as its defenders claimed, like a family, then it was only right and just that the elder members of that family be cared for in their dotage. Arthur had presided over the beginning of the end of the boss system, and in his final gesture as chief executive, he made sure that the man who had led the Republican Party for more than a decade could die with his honor and dignity intact.

Grant died in July, and Arthur did not outlive him by long. As he left the White House, he was the object of warm political eulogies. Several earlier vice presidents who had unexpectedly become president had crippled their party; John Tyler and Andrew Johnson were two notable examples still relatively fresh in people's memories. The fact that Arthur had not wrecked the Republican Party was counted in his favor. True, Blaine had lost the election, but no one could or did hold

Arthur responsible for that defeat. Arthur had become president with perilously low expectations, which he then exceeded. In essence, most people concluded that the Arthur administration hadn't been half bad. Considering that they had thought it would be all bad, Arthur was widely acclaimed for having done a respectable job.

Arthur's transition from president to private citizen was smooth. He had pined for his home in New York, and it was much as he had left it four years before. He had no difficulty finding clients and generating income. He had his choice of cases, and he didn't work too hard. In part, he wanted a respite from life in Washington, but he also began to suffer more seriously from his kidney disorder. His lethargy became progressively worse, and people started to notice that his skin was chronically gray and his eyes were drawn and exhausted. He entertained less and less, and when he did, he no longer had the appetite for drawn-out meals and celebration.

He was only fifty-six years old as 1886 began, but he was fading. In April, the *New York Times* ran an extensive article describing Arthur's Bright's disease as a fatal illness that would end his life in a matter of months. Arthur was now confined to his bed by his doctors, and he was too weak to argue. He had trouble eating solid food and was placed on a liquid diet. During the summer, he seemed to be getting better and even left the city for some weeks with his family. But when he returned from New London, Connecticut, in late September, his condition worsened. Even as he wasted away, he still wanted to see friends and talk about what was going in the world. He didn't deny what was happening to him, but he held out hope that it would pass. He lost more weight and withered to a shell of his former self by the fall. On November 18, 1886, after an artery in his brain ruptured, he died at home at 123 Lexington Avenue with his sister and son by his side and his daughter in a room nearby.

The encomiums were generous. "He died as he lived, a gentleman," said one friend. The Union League Club held a special meeting, and member after member rose to praise his character, his decency, and his modesty. A suitably grand Episcopal memorial service was held in New York, attended by senators, governors, generals, cabinet officers, by President Cleveland, former president Hayes, James G. Blaine, Roscoe Conkling, and by everyone who was anyone in New York City. After the service, his body was taken to Albany. There, in Rural Cemetery, on a ridge above the Hudson Valley, Chester Arthur was buried in his family plot, next to his wife, Ellen, and the child they had lost.

Epilogue

The Gentleman President

In the years after his death, Chester Arthur's reputation didn't rise and it didn't fall. It disappeared. Arthur was warmly eulogized, but in his own lifetime he generated almost no public passion. He didn't inspire great devotion, and he didn't cause great revulsion. Whatever answer he would have given to Machiavelli's leadership question, he was neither loved nor feared, and he wasn't hated either. He was an unexpected president during a time when no one expected much from the presidency, and in an age of low expectations he was more than satisfactory.

That is hardly a recipe for drama. Arthur has been the subject of remarkably few books, and in no textbook does he earn more than a passing reference. William Henry Harrison gets more public play than Arthur, because Harrison at least can claim the record for fewest days served as president. Garfield has gotten more attention, because Garfield was at least elected in his own right and then felled by an assassin's bullet. Arthur is, as Thomas Wolfe so keenly observed, a forgotten man, and as much as it would be tempting to revive his historical reputation and reveal a hidden Arthur of charisma, vision, dynamism, and keen intellect, the truth is more prosaic.

Chester Alan Arthur may have been the most reluctant president ever to occupy the White House. At no point in his life did he want to be president, and it is safe to say that he never dreamt of being president, not because he had a low estimation of his own abilities but because he simply didn't want the job. Before the election of 1880, Arthur had never run for public office. His career had been a succession of increasingly important appointed positions. He was most comfortable as a supporting player in party politics, and as Conkling's lieutenant he excelled. Offered the vice presidency, he of course accepted, because he had lived his life in a system that demanded service to one's party and there was no greater honor than being called on by that party. He was proud to be selected as Garfield's running mate. He was delighted that the ticket won. And he was devastated when Garfield was shot, and even more crushed to become president himself.

The three and a half years he spent in the White House were among the least pleasant of his life. Physically stretched and emotionally drained, he strove to do what was right for the country. Given his close association with faction, spoils, and party, that itself was a surprise. The office of the presidency, even in eras when the White House is not at the center of public life, seems to alter the way its primary inhabitant views the world. The president may make wise decisions or dumb decisions, but to a man, presidents have confessed to a sense that suddenly partisan pettiness is inappropriate to the office. Some have been able to transcend partisan politics more than others, and on that score Arthur is certainly among the most honorable chief executives the country has seen. He tried to serve the general good rather than the interests of his faction. Overall, he was more reactive than active. He didn't rally Congress to change the nature of the civil service, and he didn't lead the charge to build a modern navy, assert the primacy of the United States in South and Central America, or reduce tariffs. He was, however, a vital element.

So what about that nature-nurture question? Was Arthur responsible for reform, or was he just there when it happened? Was he a place holder, or did he define his place? As with much else about Arthur, the truth is less satisfying than drama demands. Another person in his shoes might have made reform a personal crusade and become synonymous with it. Another person might have succumbed to the venality of Gilded Age politics and done what he could to make all reform toothless. Arthur did for civil service reform what he had done for most things in his life: he added a note of grace and honor, and the result was a balanced piece of legislation at a time when that was rare.

He was also a voice of reason and moderation during the angry debate over Chinese immigration in 1882, and he wisely checked the worst instincts of Congress when he vetoed the pork barrel appropriation bill for rivers and harbors. The same spirit animated his cabinet appointments and infused his public speeches. The grace that he brought to politics he brought also to the Washington social scene with a glittering, renovated White House. These qualities were reflected in personal appearance as well. While he certainly enjoyed the perks of affluence, unlike Conkling he dressed the way he did not to draw attention to himself as a peacock but because he believed it added to his dignity. In fact, in his years in New York, he managed to maintain a clean reputation even as allegations of corruption surrounded him. If there is such a thing as integrity in a corrupt system, Arthur possessed it. In short, throughout his public life, Arthur conducted himself with honor at a time when politics was venal and petty.

That didn't mean that his actions were beyond reproach. He thrived in a system of assessments and paybacks, and he knew full well who Stephen Dorsey was and what was done in Indiana in 1880. Arthur was, in every way, a man of his time.

And yet there is something about him that shaped the nation during his time in office. The 1870s were marked by scandals, financial panics, and gathering labor unrest. The later 1880s witnessed violence between workers and factory owners so intense that some began to worry about the stability of the country. Arthur was hardly the most important factor in American life in these years. The swirling forces of industrialization, immigration, and western exploration shaped subsequent society more than his actions. But while Arthur was president, the country was remarkably and atypically calm. The economy was stable. The federal government took baby steps away from the spoils system and toward an ethos of "for the people, by the people," and even the Wild West started to become less wild.

It would be silly to give Arthur too much credit for this calm interregnum, but perhaps he should get more than he's gotten. Presidents who govern during a time of calm and prosperity often suffer the barbs of history. They are remembered, if at all, as bland. The calm of Arthur's presidency was an anomaly for the tumult of late-nineteenth-century America, yet it perfectly matched his temperament. In ways that his contemporaries did not recognize, Arthur set a tone that permeated the country. The tenor of the time may have been much the same without him, but all we know for certain is that it was what it was with him.

We seek greatness in our leaders, and we judge them lacking if we don't find it. Usually, that is as it should be, but sometimes, strong vision and force of character aren't required and might not be appreciated. Only Blaine among Arthur's contemporaries possessed both those qualities, but he was saddled with great weaknesses as well. Had Blaine been president, it's far from clear which side of him would have triumphed.

In everything he did, Chester Alan Arthur was a gentleman, and that is rare and precious. It reminds us that adversaries can be treated with respect, that democracy can survive differences, and that leadership isn't just great words and deeds. Arthur managed to be a decent man and a decent president in an era when decency was in short supply.

For those who want presidents to be heroes, and, failing that, villains, for those who expect them to be larger-than-life figures, Arthur's tenure in office isn't satisfying. The nature of our expectations would have to change dramatically for Arthur to be reevaluated as one of this country's best presidents. And yet, in spite of what Shakespeare wrote, some men are neither born great, nor achieve greatness, nor have it thrust upon them. Some people just do the best they can in a difficult situation, and sometimes that turns out just fine.

Milestones

1829 Chester Alan Arthur is born in North Fairfield, Vermont.

1832–33 South Carolina attempts to nullify two federal tariff bills, but is forced to back down by President Andrew Jackson.

1848 Arthur graduates from Union College in Schenectady, New York.

1850 The Compromise of 1850. California joins the Union as a free state and Congress passes a stringent Fugitive Slave Act.

1854 Arthur works as a law clerk for antislavery lawyer Erastus Culver in New York City.

1854 Congress passes the Kansas-Nebraska Act, which allows the two territories to be admitted as either a slave state or a free state depending on what their legislatures determine.

1856 Arthur moves to Kansas to support the antislavery forces, but returns to New York City a few months later to resume his law practice.

1856 The new Republican Party meets in Philadelphia and nominates John Frémont as its candidate for president.

1859 Arthur marries Ellen Lewis Herndon.

1861 South Carolina secedes from the Union; the Civil War begins.

1861–63 Arthur serves as chief engineer and then quartermaster-general of New York State under Republican governor Edwin Morgan.

1863–65 After Morgan loses the 1862 election, Arthur returns to private life and remains in New York City as a lawyer for the rest of the war.

July 1863 William Arthur, the firstborn child of Chester and Nell, dies from an infection at the age of two and a half.

1868 Republican Roscoe Conkling is elected to the U.S. Senate by the New York legislature; Ulysses S. Grant becomes the second Republican to be elected president.

1871 Due to Conkling's patronage, Arthur is appointed collector of the New York Customhouse by Grant.

1873 The Panic of 1873 sends the country into a multiyear economic depression.

1874 In a nod toward reform, Congress ends the moiety system that had allowed customs officials to reap personal gain from seized goods. As a result, Arthur's income as collector is reduced from fifty thousand dollars to twelve thousand dollars a year.

1878 Charging that the New York Customhouse had been poorly administered, President Rutherford Hayes removes Arthur as collector, which bitterly divides the Republican Party.

1879 Henry George's *Progress and Poverty* is published.

1880 At the Republican National Convention in Chicago, Ohio's James Garfield emerges as a dark-horse candidate. As a gesture toward the Stalwart wing of the party led by Conkling and Grant, Chester Arthur is asked to be Garfield's running mate.

1880 Garfield and Arthur defeat the Democratic ticket of Winfield Hancock and William English by less than one-tenth of 1 percent of votes cast.

July 2, 1881 President Garfield is shot by Charles Guiteau before boarding a train in Washington, D.C.

September 19, 1881 Garfield succumbs to his wounds and dies.

September 20, 1881 Chester Arthur is sworn in as the twenty-first president of the United States in his home in New York City.

1882 The Star Route trials begin; former Arthur ally Stephen Dorsey and others are accused of using postal routes to defraud the federal government.

April 1882 Arthur vetoes the first version of the Chinese Exclusion Act barring Chinese immigration. After some of its provisions are removed, Congress passes another version, which becomes law.

June 30, 1882 Charles Guiteau, the convicted assassin of Garfield, is hanged in Washington, D.C.

August 1882 Arthur vetoes the Rivers and Harbors Bill, claiming that the bill would help only "particular localities" rather than the general good.

September 5, 1882 In New York City, thousands of laborers parade to honor the workingman on what would later become the official holiday of Labor Day.

November 1882 On Election Day, Republicans are soundly defeated by the Democrats. They lose the gubernatorial race in New York to Grover Cleveland, and they lose control of the House of Representatives by a wide margin.

January 1883 Arthur signs the Pendleton Civil Service Act into law.

March 1883 On the urging of Arthur's secretary of the navy William Chandler, Congress funds the construction of three steel-armored cruisers.

May 1883 The Brooklyn Bridge opens in New York City.

Summer 1883 Arthur makes a trip to the West and visits Yellowstone Park.

November 1883 The Supreme Court rules the Civil Rights Act of 1875 unconstitutional.

June 1884 The Republican convention does not renominate Arthur and instead chooses James Blaine as its candidate for president.

November 4, 1884 Blaine loses the election to Democrat Grover Cleveland.

1885 Arthur returns to New York City as a private citizen.

November 18, 1886 Arthur dies at the age of fifty-seven at his home at 123 Lexington Avenue.

Selected Bibliography

Ackerman, Kenneth. *Dark Horse: The Surprise Election and Political Murder of President James A. Garfield.* New York: Carroll and Graf, 2003.

Beckert, Sven. *The Monied Metropolis: New York and the Consolidation of the American Bourgeoisie, 1850–1896.* New York: Cambridge University Press, 2001.

Brown, Dee. *The American West.* New York: Scribners, 1994.

Bryce, James. *The American Commonwealth.* New York: Macmillan, 1891.

Calhoun, Charles, ed. *The Gilded Age: Essays on the Origins of Modern America.* Wilmington: Scholarly Resources, 1996.

Chang, Iris. *The Chinese in America: A Narrative History.* New York: Viking, 2003.

Crapol, Edward. *James G. Blaine: Architect of Empire.* Wilmington: Scholarly Resources, 2000.

Daniels, Roger. *Coming to America: A History of Immigration and Ethnicity in American Life.* New York: HarperCollins, 1990.

Doenecke, Justus. *The Presidencies of James A. Garfield and Chester A. Arthur.* Lawrence: University Press of Kansas, 1981.

Foner, Eric. *Reconstruction: America's Unfinished Revolution, 1863–1877.* New York: Harper and Row, 1988.

Hoogenboom, Ari. *Outlawing the Spoils: A History of the Civil Service Reform Movement, 1865–1883.* Urbana: University of Illinois Press, 1961.

Howe, George. *Chester A. Arthur: A Quarter-Century of Machine Politics.* New York: Dodd, Mean, 1934.

Jordan, David. *Roscoe Conkling of New York.* Ithaca: Cornell University Press, 1971.

Josephson, Matthew. *The Robber Barons.* New York: Harcourt, 1934.

Keller, Morton. *Affairs of State: Public Life in Late Nineteenth Century America.* Cambridge: Belknap Press of Harvard University Press, 1977.

LaFeber, Walter. *The Cambridge History of American Foreign Relations.* Vol. 2, *The American Search for Opportunity, 1865–1913.* New York: Cambridge University Press, 1993.

Mandelbaum, Seymour. *Boss Tweed's New York.* Chicago: Ivan Dee, 1990.

Marcus, Robert. *Grand Old Party: Political Structure in the Gilded Age, 1880–1896.* New York: Oxford University Press, 1971.

Morgan, H. Wayne. *From Hayes to McKinley: National Party Politics, 1877–1896.* Syracuse: Syracuse University Press, 1969.

Peskin, Allan. *Garfield.* Kent, Ohio: Kent State University Press, 1978, 1999.

Potter, David. *The Impending Crisis, 1848–1861.* New York: Harper and Row, 1976.

Reeves, Thomas. *Gentleman Boss: The Life and Times of Chester Alan Arthur.* Newton, Conn.: American Political Biography Press, 1975, 1998.

Riordon, William. *Plunkitt of Tammany Hall: A Series of Very Plain Talks on Very Practical Politics.* New York: Knopf, 1948.

Schlereth, Thomas. *Victorian America: Transformations in Everyday Life, 1876–1915.* New York: HarperCollins, 1991.

Skowronek, Stephen. *Building a New American State: The Expansion of National Administrative Capacities, 1877–1920.* New York: Cambridge University Press, 1982.

Smith, Jean Edward. *Grant.* New York: Simon and Schuster, 2001.

Thomas, John. "Nationalizing the Republic, 1877–1920." In Bernard Bailyn et al., *The Great Republic: A History of the American People.* Lexington, Mass.: D. C. Heath, 1992.

Tractenberg, Alan. *The Incorporation of America: Culture and Society in the Gilded Age.* New York: Hill and Wang, 1982.

Trefousse, Hans. *Rutherford B. Hayes.* New York: Times Books, 2002.

Tutorow, Norman. *James Gillespie Blaine and the Presidency.* New York: Peter Lang, 1989.

Acknowledgments

Writing about a less-well-known president presented a challenge. There is a dearth of material on Chester Arthur, both because his time in office was brief and because most of his private papers were destroyed after his death. I drew on the work of his few earlier biographers, particularly George Howe, who wrote on Arthur in the 1930s; Thomas Reeves, who published what remains the most authoritative biography of Arthur in the 1970s; and Justus Doenecke, who penned a joint study of Garfield and Arthur in the early 1980s. I relied heavily on newspaper and magazine accounts from the 1870s and 1880s. Here, I drew on the invaluable help of LeeAnna Keith, who did the thankless task of reading loops of microfilm and extracting the nuggets and who helped me survey the literature not just on the presidency but also on American society during Arthur's lifetime.

Once a draft was complete, I benefited from the careful reading and wise suggestions of Arthur Schlesinger, Jr., and from the equally incisive comments of my editor, Paul Golob. I also owe thanks to Professor H. W. Brands, whose many works of history have enriched my understanding of American culture, and who generously spent some time critiquing what I had written. The logistics of publication were handled first by Heather Rodino and then by Brianna Smith at Times Books, and they helped ensure that this book would fit its tight schedule. My agent, John Hawkins, was once again a source of support, and I thank him for indulging me when I wanted to talk rather than write.

Others who have my heartfelt thanks are David Sobel, who signed me up to write the book, and Eric Foner, Ernest May, Ryland Clarke, Esty Foster, Massimo Maglione, Akira Iriye, and especially James Shenton. I learned about American history from them, and I have always cherished their passion for it. Without them, I doubt I would have developed my own fascination for how the United States has evolved. And finally, to my wife, Nicole, and my son, Griffin, who fill my days with light.

Index

ABOUT THE AUTHOR

———

ZACHARY KARABELL is the author of several works of American and world history, including *The Last Campaign: How Harry Truman Won the 1948 Election* and *Parting the Desert: The Creation of the Suez Canal.* He has taught at Harvard and Dartmouth, and his work has appeared in the *New York Times*, the *Los Angeles Times*, *Foreign Affairs*, and *Newsweek*. He lives in New York City.